Charles Stewart Parnell

HISTORICAL ASSOCIATION OF IRELAND

LIFE AND TIMES

NEW SERIES

General Editor: Ciaran Brady

Now available
Michael Davitt by Carla King
Thomas Kettle by Senia Pašeta
John Mitchel by James Quinn
Denis Guiney by Peter Costello
Frank Ryan by Fearghal McGarry
William Martin Murphy by Thomas J. Morrissey, SJ
Justin McCarthy by Eugene J. Doyle

Titles are in preparation on Sir Edward Carson,
Joseph McGrath, James Clarence Mangan
Isaac Butt and Maria Edgeworth.

Charles Stewart Parnell

ALAN O'DAY

Published on behalf of
the Historical Association of Ireland
by

UNIVERSITY COLLEGE DUBLIN PRESS
Preas Choláiste Ollscoile Bhaile Átha Cliath
2012

First published 1998 on behalf of the
Historical Association of Ireland by Dundalgan Press, Dundalk
This Second Edition first published 2012 on behalf of the
Historical Association of Ireland by
University College Dublin Press

ISBN 978–1–906359–33–1
ISSN 2009–1397

University College Dublin Press
Newman House, 86 St Stephen's Green
Dublin 2, Ireland
www.ucdpress.ie

Cataloguing in Publication data available from the British Library

Typeset in Scotland in Ehrhardt by Ryan Shiels
Text design by Lyn Davies
Printed in England on acid-free paper by
MPG Books

CONTENTS

For the Parnell Society

*

FOREWORD

Originally conceived over a decade ago to place the lives of leading figures in Irish history against the background of new research on the problems and conditions of their times and modern assessments of their historical significance, the Historical Association of Ireland Life and Times series enjoyed remarkable popularity and success. A second series has now been planned in association with UCD Press in a new format and with fuller scholarly apparatus. Encouraged by the reception given to the earlier series, the volumes in the new series will be expressly designed to be of particular help to students preparing for the Leaving Certificate, for GCE Advanced Level and for undergraduate history courses as well as appealing to the happily insatiable appetite for new views of Irish history among the general public.

CIARAN BRADY
Historical Association of Ireland

PREFACE

The opportunity to rework and largely rewrite my pamphlet owes much to people, past and present. I wish to thank especially Peter Alter, Walter Arnstein, Paul Bew, John Broad, George Boyce, Miles Bradbury, Mike Bromley, Penny Cookson, Dennis Dean, David Fitzpatrick, Neil Fleming, Sheridan Gilley, Terry Gourvish, David Howell, Michael Hurst, Liam Kennedy, Carla King, Donal Lowry, Gerard McCoy, Anne Mouron, James H. Murphy, Andrew Sean Dominic O'Day, Roland Quinault, Lord Skidelsky, John Stevenson, Charles Thomas, F. M. L. Thompson, Bill Vaughan, Jon Wakelyn, B. M. Walker, Fr Tom Weinandy along with the editors of the series. Patrick Maume offered advice on an earlier revision and Paul Bew permitted me to read the proofs of his fine biography of Parnell. Noelle Moran and Barbara Mennell at the University College Dublin Press pushed the project forward. I received funding from the British Academy, National Endowment for the Humanities, and Nuffield Foundation. During the long gestation I spent periods at Linacre, Mansfield, St Antony's, St John's and Wolfson Colleges and the Rothermere American Institute, all in the University of Oxford, St Aidan's College in the University of Durham, the Institute for Advanced Studies in the Humanities at the University of Edinburgh, the Catholic University of America, the School of Advanced Study at the University of London, Trinity College Dublin, Institute of Irish Studies, Queen's University Belfast, and Greyfriars Hall, University of Oxford.

ALAN O'DAY
14 March 2012

CHRONOLOGY OF PARNELL'S LIFE AND TIMES

1846
27 June: Charles Stewart Parnell born to John Henry and Delia Tudor Stewart Parnell, at Avondale, County Wicklow.

1853
Attends school at Yeovil, Somerset in England.

1859
3 July: Death of father; Parnell inherits Avondale and is made ward of chancery.

1865
October: Matriculates at Magdalene College, Cambridge.

1867
June: Parnell reaches his majority and takes possession of Avondale.

1868
17 November–2 December: General election (Gladstone appointed Liberal Prime Minister on 3 December; Chichester S. Fortescue appointed Chief Secretary; Earl Spencer sworn as Lord Lieutenant on 18 December).

1869
26 May: Parnell sent down from Cambridge following a brawl.

1870
19 May: private meeting at Bilton Hotel, Dublin, marks founding of Home Rule movement.

1871

12 January: Marquess of Hartington appointed Chief Secretary in succession to Fortescue. *Spring:* Parnell departs for America.

1872

January: Parnell returns from the United States.

1873

18–21 November: National Conference establishes Home Rule League. *Winter:* Parnell, High Sheriff of County Wicklow.

1874

31 January–12 February: general election (60 Home Rulers returned); *7 February:* John Howard Parnell bottom of the poll in County Wicklow. *20 February:* Disraeli appointed Prime Minister (created Earl of Beaconsfield, 21 August 1876). *27 February:* Sir Michael Hicks Beach appointed Chief Secretary. *3 March:* Irish Parliamentary Party founded. *18 March:* Charles Stewart Parnell defeated in Dublin County by-election (2,183–1,235).

1875

13 January: Gladstone retires as Liberal party leader. *29 March:* John Martin, MP for County Meath, dies. *19 April:* Parnell wins County Meath by-election (1,771–1,050 for two opponents combined). *22 April:* Parnell takes his seat. *26 April:* Parnell makes maiden speech in the House of Commons.

1876

30 June–1 July: Home Rule debate in House of Commons (*30 June:* Parnell says that no murder was committed at Manchester in 1867). *November:* Parnell travels to the United States for the centenary of American independence. *12 December:* Duke of Marlborough sworn in as Lord Lieutenant.

1877

27 July–1 August: Parnell and Joseph Biggar spearhead obstruction. *27–28 August:* annual convention of the Home Rule League of Great Britain held at Liverpool; Parnell elected President for the next year.

1878

14–15 January: Home Rule conference meets to consider parliamentary policy where Parnell pledges support for Isaac Butt if the party leader pursued an 'active strategy'. *15 February:* James Lowther succeeds Hicks Beach as Chief Secretary. *12 May:* Parnell declines Michael Davitt's invitation to join the Irish Republican Brotherhood (IRB). *21–22 October:* Parnell re-elected president of the Home Rule Confederation of Great Britain at its annual convention. *27 October:* John Devoy offers Parnell support of Fenians. *3 November:* Parnell addresses meeting of the Ballinasloe Tenants' Defence Association in his first visit to Connaught.

1879

7–9 March: Parnell has discussions with John Devoy and John O'Leary on the proposed 'New Departure'. *6 April:* Parnell meets Devoy and Michael Davitt concerning the possibility of a 'New Departure'. *20 April:* Tenant Right Association meeting at Irishtown, County Mayo. *5 May:* Butt dies. *22 May:* William Shaw elected party chairman. *1 June:* Parnell meets John Devoy and Michael Davitt, resulting in the 'New Departure'. *8 June:* Parnell speaks at Westport, County Mayo land meeting where he states 'hold a firm grip of your homestead and lands'. *26 July:* Parnell's candidate, James Lysaght Finigan, wins Ennis by-election (83–77). *16 August:* National Land League of Mayo founded. *29 September:* 'Appeal to the Irish Race' by Parnell and Michael Davitt seeks aid of the diaspora in new land agitation. *21 October:* Irish National Land League founded; Parnell elected President. *21 December:* Parnell and John Dillon sail to North America.

1880

2 January: Parnell arrives in New York. *2 February:* addresses American House of Representatives. *20 February:* when speaking at Cincinnati, Ohio, is alleged to have called for breaking the 'last link' between Ireland and Britain (he would deny using this phrase). *8 March:* government announces dissolution of parliament. *11 March:* Parnell initiates the Irish National Land and Industrial League of the United States (American Land League). *21 March:* Parnell returns to Ireland. *31 March–13 April:* general election; Parnell returned for Cork City (5 April), County Meath (10 April) and County Mayo (12 April), choosing to sit for Cork City (overall, 63 Home Rulers elected); *23 April:* Gladstone appointed Prime Minister; *30 April:* W. E. Forster appointed Chief Secretary; *5 May:* Earl Cowper sworn in as Lord Lieutenant. *18 April:* Bishop Thomas Nulty authorises church-door collection to defray Parnell's election expenses. *17 May:* Parnell elected sessional chairman of Irish Parliamentary Party (23–18). *30 July:* Parnell meets Katharine O'Shea for the first time. *19 September:* Parnell's speech at Ennis advocates what becomes known as 'boycotting'. *24 October:* Parnell's 'coats off' speech at Galway. *2 November:* 14 leaders of the Land League (including Parnell) indicted for conspiracy to prevent payment of rent – trial begins 28 December, collapses on 25 January 1881 when jury fails to reach verdict.

1881

13–18 February: Parnell in France where he meets with Land League leaders and visits French radicals. *7 September:* Thomas A. Dickson, the Liberal candidate, wins the County Tyrone by-election, while Parnell's candidate polls weakly. *15–17 September:* Land League convention adopts Parnell's formula to 'test' the Land Act. *7 October:* Gladstone at Leeds states that 'resources of civilisation' not exhausted. *9 October:* Parnell speaks at Wexford in reply to Gladstone's address at Leeds. *13 October:* Parnell imprisoned without trial under the provisions of the Protection of Person and Property Act. *18 October:* 'No Rent Manifesto'. *19 October:* 'No Rent Manifesto' denounced by Archbishop

Thomas Croke. *20 October:* Land Court opens; government suppresses Land League.

1882

Parnell free on parole. *28 April:* Lord Cowper resigns as Lord Lieutenant (Earl Spencer sworn in 6 May). *2 May:* released from Kilmainham jail under the compact known as the 'Kilmainham Treaty'; W. E. Forster resigns as Chief Secretary (replaced by Lord Frederick Cavendish on 6 May). *6 May:* Cavendish and Thomas Burke, Under-Secretary, murdered in Phoenix Park – in the aftermath the police watch Parnell, whose relationship with Katharine O'Shea is reported to the Home Secretary and via him to the cabinet. *9 May:* George Otto Trevelyan appointed Chief Secretary. *16 August:* Parnell receives the Freedom of Dublin. *17 October:* Irish National League founded.

1883

3 March: National Tribute begun for Parnell who faced foreclosure on Avondale. *17 March:* Archbishop Thomas Croke subscribes £50 to Parnell Testimonial. *11 May:* National Tribute for Parnell condemned by Vatican. *30 June:* T. M. Healy wins Monaghan by-election (2,376–2,001), where Parnell campaigns on his behalf. *4 July:* Parnell receives the Freedom of Cork. *11 December:* Parnell presented with testimonial of more than £37,000 from the National Tribute.

1884

1 October: Irish Catholic hierarchy formally requests Irish Party to represent its education interests in the House of Commons. *23 October:* Sir Henry Campbell-Bannerman appointed Chief Secretary in succession to George Otto Trevelyan. *23 November:* Captain William H. O'Shea gives note to Joseph Chamberlain purporting to be Parnell's view on renewal of the Crimes Act. *1 December:* Redistribution Bill introduced in House of Commons (enacted 25 June 1885; eliminates 22 small boroughs in Ireland). *6 December:* Representation of the People Act (Irish electorate increased from 126,000 to 738,000).

1885

9 January: John O'Connor returns unopposed at Tipperary parliamentary by-election (Parnell went to county to support candidacy when an initial convention selected another man; the convention was declared unrepresentative); Parnell receives the Freedom of Clonmel. *15 January:* Memorandum by Captain O'Shea, written 14 January 'Local Self-Government', purporting to have Parnell's approval is given to Joseph Chamberlain. *21 January:* Parnell speaks at Cork where he says 'no man has the right to fix the boundary to the march of a nation'. *9 May:* Joseph Chamberlain's scheme for Irish local government is rejected by the cabinet though it has Gladstone's support. *20 May:* Lord Randolph Churchill states that a Conservative ministry would not renew the Crimes Act. *9 June:* Liberal government resigns after a defeat in the House of Commons; *23 June:* Lord Salisbury appointed Prime Minister; *25 June:* Sir William Hart Dyke appointed Chief Secretary; *27 June:* Edward Gibson created Lord Ashbourne on becoming Lord Chancellor of Ireland. *30 June:* Earl of Carnarvon sworn as Lord Lieutenant. *1 August:* Parnell has secret meeting with Lord Carnarvon. *20 August:* Arklow, County Wicklow, where he spoke in favour of protection. *25 August* and *1 September:* Parnell makes major pronouncements on the forthcoming election, defining his position as 'one plank of home rule' in the coming general election. *5 October:* At first National League convention to select parliamentary candidates held in County Wicklow, Parnell emphasises the 'single plank' of Home Rule. *10 November:* At Liverpool Parnell seeks a declaration from Gladstone on Home Rule (Gladstone declines on 17 November). *21 November:* Irish National League of Great Britain manifesto urges the Irish in Britain to vote against the Liberals and Radicals. *22–24 November:* Parnell campaigns on behalf of Captain William H. O'Shea in Liverpool. *23 November–9 December:* general election; Liberals returned with largest number of MPs (335), which is exactly equalled by the total of Conservatives (249) and Home Rulers (86). *17 December:* Herbert Gladstone announces that his father is converted to Home Rule ('Hawarden Kite').

1886

12 January: Parliament opens; Lord Carnarvon resigns. *23 January:* W. H. Smith succeeds Sir William Hart Dyke as Chief Secretary. *26 January:* Conservative Ministry defeated in the House of Commons (329–250) on Queen's Speech which proposes to restore coercion in Ireland. *28 January:* Salisbury's ministry resigns; *1 February:* Gladstone appointed Prime Minister; *6 February:* John Morley appointed Chief Secretary. *1–10 February:* Galway City by-election Captain O'Shea returned (942–54). *10 February:* Parnell's last public speech in Ireland until December 1890; Earl of Aberdeen sworn in as Lord Lieutenant. *5 April:* Parnell meets with Gladstone and Morley to discuss financial aspects of Home Rule. *8 April:* Government of Ireland Bill [Home Rule] introduced in House of Commons. *17 April:* Land Purchase Bill introduced in House of Commons (withdrawn 11 June). *8 June:* Government of Ireland Bill defeated on its second reading in the House of Commons (341–311). *26 June:* parliament dissolved; *1–17 July:* general election in which Irish Party wins 85 seats but Conservatives and Liberal Unionists capture a majority; *25 July:* Salisbury appointed Prime Minister; *5 August:* Sixth Marquess of Londonderry sworn as Lord Lieutenant and Sir Michael Hicks Beach appointed Chief Secretary. *18 August:* General Sir Redvers Buller appointed as temporary Special Commissioner for Counties Kerry and Clare. *20 September:* Parnell's Tenants' Relief Bill defeated in the House of Commons. *23 October:* Plan of Campaign published in *United Ireland*. *c.9–10 December:* Parnell meets William O'Brien behind Greenwich Observatory to discuss the Plan of Campaign. *18 December:* Plan of Campaign proclaimed 'an unlawful and criminal conspiracy'.

1887

7 March: Arthur Balfour becomes Chief Secretary in succession to Sir Michael Hicks Beach; *The Times* begins series 'Parnellism and Crime' (also 10, 14 March, 18 April, 13 May, 1 December). *18 April:* facsimile letter purported to be Parnell's approving of the assassination of T. H. Burke on 6 May 1882 published in *The Times*. *20 July:* Parnell addresses the National Liberal Club. *19 August:* National League proclaimed as a 'dangerous association'. *15 October:* Sir Joseph West Ridgeway appointed Under-Secretary.

1888

20 April: Papal Rescript condemns Plan of Campaign and boycotting. *8 May:* Parnell addresses the Liberal 80 Club and dissociates himself from Plan of Campaign. *5 July:* verdict against F. H. O'Donnell in suit against *The Times* over the articles 'Parnellism and Crime'. *20 July:* Parnell speaks at a meeting of the National Liberal Club. *6 August:* Parnell's letter in *The Times* dated 4 August explains negotiations with Joseph Chamberlain in late 1884 and early 1885 on local self-government in Ireland. *13 August:* Special Commission on 'Parnellism and Crime' established. *17 September–22 November 1889:* Special Commission, Parnellism and Crime.

1889

20–22 February: Richard Pigott unmasked as forger of letters published in *The Times* (commits suicide in Madrid on 1 March). *30 Apr.–8 May:* Parnell testifies before Special Commission. *8 May:* Parnell speaks at the National Liberal Club. *19 May:* Mrs Benjamin Wood dies leaving most of her estate to Mrs Katharine O'Shea (the will is contested by other relatives). *5 October:* Earl of Zetland sworn as Lord Lieutenant. *18–19 December:* Parnell is Gladstone's guest at Hawarden, where they discuss the future Home Rule Bill; *24 December:* Captain William H. O'Shea files a petition for divorce, naming Parnell as co-respondent. *30 December:* Parnell in an interview published in the *Freeman's Journal* explains that he has lived at the O'Shea residence for several years.

1890

January: Numerous public bodies in Ireland express confidence in Parnell. *17 November:* O'Shea granted a decree *nisi* in his divorce petition. *20 November:* Parnell's leadership endorsed by meeting held in Leinster Hall, Dublin; *20–21 November:* National Liberal Federation expresses strong feelings against Parnell. *24 November:* Gladstone meets Justin McCarthy and undertakes to continue the fight for Home Rule, though without hope of success. *25 November:* Parnell unanimously re-elected chairman of Irish Party. *26 November:* Gladstone publishes letter to Morley, stating that if Parnell remains as leader of Irish Party, his own leadership will be 'almost a nullity'. *29 November:* publication of Parnell's manifesto 'To the People of Ireland'. *30 November:* John Dillon, William O'Brien, T. P. O'Connor, T. P. Gill and T. D. Sullivan on a fund-raising tour in America repudiate Parnell's leadership. *1–6 December:* Irish Party meets in Committee Room 15, Palace of Westminster, and splits on the 6th, when 45 MPs withdraw to form an anti-Parnellite grouping, leaving behind 28 Parnellites. *3 December:* standing committee of the Irish Catholic hierarchy denounces Parnell. *10 December:* Parnell arrives in Dublin and receives a hero's welcome. *11 December:* Anti-Parnellite manifesto by Justin McCarthy published in *Freeman's Journal*. *20 December:* Parnell's leadership endorsed by meeting held in Leinster Hall, Dublin. *22 December:* anti-Parnellite candidate, Sir John Pope Hennessy, wins North Kilkenny by-election (2,527–1,362). *30 December:* negotiations between William O'Brien and Parnell begin in Boulogne (terminate without agreement, 11 February 1891).

1891

10 January: Limerick City Parnell begins a series of public meetings defending his position, extending to 4 April. *12 February:* following breakdown of Boulogne negotiations Dillon and O'Brien land at Folkestone in order to be rearrested and imprisoned. *4 March*: Clerkenwell, London, Parnell speaks on labour question. *14 March:* Labour conference, Dublin Parnell supported the claims of labour. *2 April:* anti-Parnellite candidate wins Sligo North by-election (3,261–2,493). *7 June:* Inchicore, County Dublin, Parnell issues a pronouncement on social policy. *17 June:* Bermondsey, London, Parnell makes a significant address supporting land purchase legislation. *25 June:* Parnell and Katharine O'Shea marry. *27 June:* Parnell's 45th birthday. *8 July:* anti-Parnellite candidate wins Carlow by-election (3,755–1,539). *18 July:* Town Hall, Newcastle upon Tyne, England, where Parnell makes a major speech on the Irish policy and home rule. *30 July:* on their release from prison, William O'Brien and John Dillon declare against Parnell. *20 September:* Cabinteely, County

Dublin, he spoke at a registration meeting in favour of 'one man, one vote'. *21 September: Freeman's Journal* declares against Parnell. *27 September:* Parnell's last public speech at Creggs, County Roscommon. *6 October:* Parnell dies. *11 October:* funeral, with burial in Glasnevin cemetery attended by over 100,000 people.

1911

1 October: Parnell monument in Dublin unveiled.

CHAPTER I

The Makings of a Nationalist

INTRODUCTION

Charles Stewart Parnell is a seminal figure in British and Irish history. There have been many attempts to illuminate his life. This short study has the objects of making him accessible to a general, as well as a specialist, audience, and placing him in the context of a modern literature and theoretical perspectives. What emerges is both familiar and distinct. It mines Parnell's public and parliamentary speeches. These speeches are the only substantial source for his political vision and reveal a philosophical and social outlook that marked him out from the mainstream of Irish nationalists in his own era and later. The main themes pursued here are:

- His essential ingredient was charisma which rendered him largely indifferent to organisational structures;
- Parnell was not an enigma: his outlook is explained by inheritance, social situation, and personal finances;
- He subscribed to liberal Protestant and Victorian democratic values and believed in the virtues of parliamentary institutions which taken together formed a cornerstone to his interpretation of the Constitution;
- He believed that Ireland's ailments resulted from English colonialism; even when colonialism had abated, its legacy – post-colonialism – continued to plague development;

- Parnell held a particular view of 'the nation';
- He espoused a socially progressive agenda;
- His appeal to physical force nationalists was the consequence of a recognised mutual empathy resulting from compatible views of 'the nation', the country's position as a consequence of English colonialism, his professed admiration of men who were prepared to win rights through the armed struggle and shared attitudes to social issues.

Parnell, a Protestant landlord, is frequently portrayed as an anomaly leading a mainly Catholic anti-Ascendancy nationalism. This is misleading. The Home Rule movement at the time Parnell enlisted was still a cross-religious pan-class grouping, and, in the broader European context, nationalist leaders drawn from the ruling strata were prominent. His fidelity remained to an all-encompassing nation. Irish nationalism was part of a fervour that shook the foundations of Europe between 1789 and the Second World War. The influences shaping Parnell's politics, ancestral tradition, maternal Anglophobia, English schooling and the Fenian rebellion, are rehearsed in older accounts of his career. Unfortunately, there is only a limited amount of direct testimony about his early life; reminiscences by contemporaries and family members were concocted later with an eye to posterity. Parnell himself wrote few letters and did not leave an account of his life. There is no Parnell archive. The principal original source for his ideas is published speeches, but these bring little enlightenment to a Parnell biography prior to his public life. His one additional medium of communication was the telegraph; he was a compulsive user but the voluminous brief messages Parnell sent contribute little. Nevertheless, using a variety of sources, the theme of the present narrative is that Parnell was a combination of family and psychological influences filtered through a political, economic and sociological ideology which gave him a hold on people in his own age and later popular consciousness. Max Weber gives attention to modes of authority.[1] Parnell fits his model of a figure exerting authority through extraordinary qualities. As Weber observes, charismatic leadership arises from a uniquely personal response to a crisis but, when the crisis passes, either the followers desert him or they seek to transmute the leader's authority into bureaucratic structures for dealing with everyday problems. The Irish national movement under Parnell is consistent with Weber's paradigms.

Much modern literature has adopted the view that Parnell was essentially a political and social conservative; here it is argued that he was a genuine Victorian liberal or Radical. Like many Radicals he was no democrat in his social relations; Parnell believed in the innate superiority of those bred to the higher station of life. However, he advocated state responsibility for the less fortunate and subscribed to the touchstone liberal value of removing barriers blocking man from rising to his potential. He believed that the leaders of the nation required the endorsement of the people: politics for him ultimately was about the organisation and pre-sentation of the parliamentary community in such a way that the passions of a virulent Catholic nationalism could be tamed. His refusal to recognise the right of the parliamentary party to depose him in 1890 stemmed from a conviction that his leadership had been conferred by the nation and only it could remove him. Parnell, perhaps because he, as a landlord, understood the avarice of the stronger tenant farmers, defended smallholders and agri-cultural labourers against them.

A further dimension of the survey is employment of theoretical insights that assist in dissecting Parnell's situation. Overall, he is distinguishable from his Irish political contemporaries. He posses-sed an unrivalled charisma. Describing the partly irrational appeal of any figure is never straightforward: it is the exceptional and unusual that marked out Parnell. Because none of his political colleagues possessed this quality, they found it impossible to command the affection, devotion and loyalty of the people after his fall.

The first of the elements making up his character – family origin – is well documented. Thomas Parnell purchased an estate in the Queen's County and moved to Ireland at the time of the Restoration in the seventeenth century. At his death a brother, John, inherited the estate. John sat in the Irish House of Commons, eventually becoming a baronet and judge. His second son, Henry, born in 1744, also served in the Irish House of Common, commanding a corps of Volunteers whose existence helped win the 'constitution of 1782'. In 1785 he became Chancellor of the Exchequer, a post he held for fourteen years. In 1799 he opposed the Union with Great Britain and was dismissed from office. Henry, who like Sir John opposed the Union, inherited the estate on his father's death in 1801, and was an MP at Westminster for many years where he supported Catholic Emancipation. He was Secretary for War in Earl Grey's cabinet between 1830 and 1832, subsequently holding office again as Paymaster General from 1835 to 1841.

The third of Sir John's sons, William, born in 1777, became the first of the family to reside at Avondale. The estate passed to Sir John in 1795 through a family connection. William Parnell twice sat in the Westminster House of Commons. His pamphlets, *An Enquiry into the Cause of Popular Discontents in Ireland* (1805) and *Historical Apology for Irish Catholics* (1807), showed sensitivity to Irish problems and a thirst for reform. He died in 1821 leaving two children, including one son, John Henry, Charles's father. According to R. F. Foster, William's writings probably had a major influence on his grandson.[2] It is unknown whether Charles read his forebears' pamphlets, but it is reasonable to assume that he was cognisant of and agreed with their liberal Protestant ethic. Although Parnell had little public taste for religion, he was a member of the Synod of the Church of Ireland, and a strong affinity for the Plymouth Brethren coursed through some parts of his kinship network.

John Henry Parnell, who was educated at Eton and Trinity College Cambridge, inherited Avondale and a long lease from Trinity College, Dublin, on land at Collure in County Armagh. Through marriage the Parnells had close ties with leading families in County Wicklow. In 1835 John Henry married Delia Stewart of a prominent American family. John Henry did not engage in national politics, though, as befitting a man of his station, he shouldered a share of unpaid local administration. There were a total of eleven children (excluding one stillborn) of the marriage. Although Charles had a comfortable and apparently happy childhood, especially at Avondale, his later contact with the majority of the siblings and mother was intermittent. He was close to John Howard, Emily Parnell Dickinson, her husband and Fanny. Parnell's mother and two sisters, including Fanny, lived in the United States for much of his public career. A younger son, Charles was born into the section of the Ascendancy that exalted its patriotic past. On entering politics, he was not bashful about claiming this legacy. Perhaps the penetrating element of his ideological inheritance was an eclectic liberalism and a sense of noblesse oblige.

Amongst Charles's assets was a towering physical presence. Three factors influenced his psychological make-up: Hayes's death in 1853 elevating Charles's situation within the patriarchal family; the death of his father in 1859; and schooling in England until he left the University of Cambridge [Magdalene College] in 1869. In 1858 John Henry purchased a substantial estate in County Carlow. The land in Armagh went to John Howard, Avondale to Charles and the

Carlow property to Henry, the youngest son. Acquisition of the
Carlow property imposed a heavy mortgage on the Avondale
estate. Avondale consisted of less than 5,000 acres and had an
income of approximately £2,000 in 1869. This places the estate
among those the smaller Irish holdings often vulnerable to
indebtedness in the years after 1878. Delia Stewart, who possibly
had not lived routinely at Avondale for several years, and her
younger children vacated the house, living from 1860 in a variety
of places, including Kingstown, Dublin and Paris, before she
returned to America in 1869. After Charles came of age in 1867,
while an undergraduate at Cambridge, he was obliged to spend
much of his time in Ireland dealing with the financial plight of his
property. The railway allowed easy access to Avondale; Parnell
spent considerable time there until the later 1880s.[3]

Family background affected Parnell's siblings in varying ways.
Two sisters were considerably more radical than Parnell; his older
brother was a loyal follower though remaining outside Ireland for
most of Charles's political career; while Henry Tudor attended
Cambridge University, lived in England and voted Tory. Some of
Charles's female siblings were apolitical. An English education
allegedly heightened his antipathy to England. Like much else,
this should be treated with reserve. In 1886 at Plymouth, Parnell
made a point of praising 'the very excellent teaching which I
received in my earlier years – to which I shall always look back with
the greatest reverence, affection, and respect . . . in the neigh-
bouring county of Somerset'.[4] Ged Martin reveals that Parnell's
ruptured undergraduate period at Cambridge resulted from ab-
sences when dealing with the Avondale estate.[5] Parnell enjoyed a
friendly relationship with his college and looked forward to re-
suming his studies. Cambridge has been described as intellectually
sterile though this, even if true, skirts the purpose then of attending
the ancient universities which first and foremost was social. What

does emerge from his Cambridge experience is an icy feistiness that would serve Parnell well. Although it is doubtful that he took much notice of Fenianism in the 1860s,[6] Parnell consistently lauded men of action who stood up for Ireland. Parnell's bond with Fenianism had genuine roots – there is some family identification with it, he had an instinctive empathy for its combativeness, anti-sectarianism, and a shared social diagnosis. Oliver P. Rafferty perceptively observes: 'nations, like individuals, are not simply the product of material circumstances. Often those at the extremes of society can, perhaps even in spite of themselves, provide a more penetrating understanding of the forces that shape public consciousness than individuals engaged in more conventional pursuits.'[7] The social base of Fenianism – displaced or threatened artisans, farm labourers and a frustrated intelligentsia – saw Ireland through a prism that paralleled Parnell's profound assessment that the problem stemmed from the colonial relationship which led to forms of human exploitation, repression and dependency. At the same time he shared with Fenians a concern that new forms of economic and cultural oppression were reinforcing colonialism – capitalist agriculture especially cattle ranching, the Catholic clergy, moneylenders and shopkeepers – and threatening the fabric of an inclusive nation. In recent decades he has been described as a constitutionalist walking a tightrope between moderate and physical force nationalists, but this is too mechanistic. Parnell was respected and supported by nationalists of the insurrectionary mode because he was genuinely sympathetic to them, if personally a committed parliamentarian. There is no inconsistency in this duality. There is another feature of Parnell's life that deviates from what is usual. He seems to have retained few friends from his youth and, excepting less than a handful of political colleagues, did not forge close relationships with his associates. Although Parnell spent many hours in the Houses of Parliament, he was not attracted by the convivial

side of politics that infatuated nationalist members. Only Katharine
O'Shea penetrated the shield.

There have been numerous attempts to discover Parnell's political,
social and economic ideas. Foster identifies the progressive character of a sector of the east Wicklow gentry as the touchstone,[8] but
Parnell had uncertain exposure to Wicklow culture. Paul Bew is
more convincing, arguing that Parnell believed that Ireland should
be governed by men of quality who lived there.[9] Tony Claydon
gives this insight muscle, maintaining that Parnell had a commitment to 'country' or 'Atlantic' principles and a belief in the
morally uplifting qualities of self-government which should be
administered close to home.[10] Parnell's support for construction
projects in Wicklow Town and Arklow illustrates perceived self-
interest coupled to a firm belief in local initiative, albeit community
self-help underwritten by state loans for development. Frank
Callanan notes that he coupled in a distinctive way *laissez-faire*
economic views with a belief in assertive governance.[11] Ironically,
the democracy he eulogised would upend him.

Parnell's economic motif has received less attention but is an
extension of his thinking. He was an unconventional landlord,
taking little interest in agricultural affairs but having a consistent
fascination with the exploitation of the natural resources and
manufacturing on his estate. A visit to Avondale quickly establishes its restricted scope for maximising agricultural income, but
the estate is forested, located in an area with mining prospects and
possessing an historic role of mineral exploitation and small-scale
industry. Parnell's ideas on economic development were linked to
the prospects of his own estate. Parnell belonged to the approximately one per cent of landlords with significant non-agricultural

economic pursuits though these may have played a considerable part in his financial undoing. Parnell's critique of cattle ranching and large-scale tenant-farmers, coupled to his support for internal emigration, improved conditions for agricultural labourers and his sympathy for industry workers can be traced to the nature of Avondale. Still, Parnell was not entirely friendly to industry action (strikes); although paying high wages he was to experience problems with labourers in his slate works. As Miroslav Hroch observes, patriotic activism took place with the growth of capitalist mechanisms of exchange.[12] Parnell, if a product of traditional Ascendancy culture, was at the cutting edge of an economically modernising Ireland.

Parnell appeared on the scene under fortuitous circumstances. Michael Hechter introduces a core-periphery analysis – the core, in this instance England, exploits the periphery, Ireland.[13] Ethnic solidarity, he contends, arises in regions developed as internal colonies where there is a hierarchical cultural division of labour determining life's chances. Liam Kennedy points out that Parnell believed that Ireland's economic backwardness was a consequence of the colonial relationship with Great Britain.[14] This verdict is sustained by Callanan, who suggests Parnell 'saw Ireland not as pre-industrial society but as one whose industrial development had been disrupted'.[15] Parnell's views on the land question constituted a resource interpretation – he urged the economic and social virtues of peasant owner-occupiers, a far from universally endorsed view amongst nationalists, advocated the claims of cottiers and agricultural labourers, and addressed the twin problems of poverty and emigration. He argued that self-government could remedy Ireland's economic deficits. Setting him apart from both fellow landlords and the majority of nationalists was a commitment to protection of manufacturers struggling against outside competition. Kennedy observes that Parnell envisaged a specialised industrial structure. Parnell's position separated him from the industrialists of Ulster, who were engaged in export-led enterprise, and his nationalist bedfellows who, if often urban men, focused mainly on land tenure. Similarly, Parnell's thinking on social structure differed; he believed that the landed classes were the natural leaders of society. If the land and national questions were resolved, his order would once again assume its place at the head of the nation. Callanan, though, posits the important reminder that Parnell's objective 'was the establishment of a viable, economically pluralistic Irish state: the conservation of a residential Anglo-Irish landlord class was instrumental, rather than promoted by an atavistic allegiance to class'.[16] By and large the implicit agenda of the Catholic national movement he headed was the displacement of a Protestant and landowning Ascendancy.

BEFORE POLITICS

After being sent down from Cambridge in May 1869 for the remainder of the university term following a youthful brawl, Charles returned to Avondale. But he did not go back to Cambridge; in the spring of 1871 he joined his older brother, John Howard, who had settled in America, on an extended tour of their mother's homeland, returning home in January 1872. Impetus for this transatlantic gambit arose from Parnell's pursuit of an American bride, a woman he met in Paris, and hope of investing a substantial sum of money abroad; both came to nought. Their travels took them mostly through the south where John Howard owned a successful peach farm. The brothers neither spent much time in centres of Irish immigration nor sought out Irish-Americans.

Prior to the beginning of 1874 Parnell's Irish experience was circumscribed by the region surrounding Avondale–Dublin and a social circle drawn from his own class. He displayed no public interest in politics though he was already a Justice of the Peace and, at merely 28, High Sheriff of County Wicklow. The accretions of youth were a marked upper-class English accent, an interest in horses, hunting and cricket, and the manners of a gentleman. No doubt his background reinforced the presumption of natural authority leading to the sense of effortless superiority that contributed to his rise to head the home rule movement and certainly was a vital strand in his reluctance to surrender leadership to lesser men in 1890–1. It is usual to note that Parnell took little interest in intellectual preoccupations; but he did have an appetite for science and mechanics. Because Parnell's English characteristics were so evident, he, his family and supporters were subsequently eager to authenticate an alleged youthful commitment to national ideals. Yet if the Parnell's patriotic credentials were not exactly exceptional, he understandably chose to stress nationalism in early forays into politics. There is an additional aspect to Parnell that has received little attention; he expected to be taken seriously by the British political elite.

CHAPTER 2

Political Apprentice, 1874–6

POLITICAL BEGINNINGS

In early 1874 Parnell made his initial effort to enter Parliament when he attempted to secure the nomination to contest County Wicklow at the general election. He was ineligible because, as High Sheriff of the county, he was responsible for conducting polling. John Howard Parnell became the surrogate candidate. The Home Rule League in Dublin was surprised to discover that the candidate professed Home Rule principles. As yet, no Parnell had joined the League or given notice of self-government ideals. At this stage the Home Rule League was a voluntary association not an organised party and played only a limited part in adopting parliamentary candidates. 'Home Ruler' was a self-selected political designation. In the event, John Howard finished bottom of the poll. Nevertheless, the campaign fired Charles's ambition and the newly formed Home Rule League lost no time enlisting so prized a recruit. Isaac Butt sought to gain the adherence of the right sort of person for Home Rule principles, most especially members of the Protestant landed class. Weber identifies three forms of authority and domination.[1] Parnell, like other Ascendancy recruits to Home Rule represented the second, traditional domination based on a belief that the legitimacy of authority has always existed and subjects obey out of personal loyalty. Later this would be replaced by Weber's third form – charismatic domination. At this juncture the home rulers fit Hroch's framework of national movements before mass mobilisation.[2] The movement retained an elite leadership, often drawn from groups not part of the mass ethnic cohort, which sought to widen the national programme to a self-government objective. Parnell's early political involvement has several significant aspects:

- He entertained parliamentary ambitions from an early point;
- He proved an adept learner;
- He held a view on the utility of parliamentary participation;
- His understanding of the land question and its resolution would allow the landed class to assume leadership of the 'nation';
- He grasped the integral relationship between home rule and social reform;
- His notion of the 'nation' embraced physical force nationalism.

Yet there remains some difficulty in determining what turned Parnell's aspiration towards parliamentary adventures. Like his father, he had obtained the expected local responsibilities though he was an inactive magistrate. Moreover, significant political involvement was certain to be a drain on his financial resources. Foster points out that Avondale, with the many charges against its income, had a narrow working margin, leaving Charles with comparative little money at his disposal.[3] And, according to Foster, the fiscal problem that left the estate in precarious order a few years afterwards was apparent by 1872 and reared its head in no uncertain way from 1875.

In March 1874 Parnell contested the County Dublin parliamentary by-election in the Home Rule interest, agreeing to pay his own election expenses that amounted to no less than £1,000 and possibly £2,000. His campaign did not fill observers with visions of the inchoate leader. His repute as a poor speaker largely dates from this and other beginning efforts. Although Parnell was ill suited to the public arena and certainly never an orator in the classic mode, in time he became a competent speaker and in the House of Commons a considerable figure. This was of no small importance, for he tailored his appearance to fit what he did effectively while eschewing as far as possible formats where he showed up less well. Parnell was ready to use family background to advantage, but this was not his only claim to support. At Kingstown Parnell showed a clearly conceived notion of the purposes of domestic self-government:

> As regarded his principles, he put Home Rule first; because it embodied everything else. He thought it comprised everything that Irishmen wished for; because when they had Home Rule they would be able to make those laws for which the country had been yearning for years. When they considered the matter fairly, what they asked for, the privilege of governing themselves, was very little. He believed when they got Home Rule – and he was certain they would get some part of it before long – they should have their manufactures encouraged; they should have their fisheries developed; they should have their gentry living at home and spending their money amongst them, and coming forward on the public platform to represent the liberties of the country.[4]

His words contained a wider-ranging analysis of the detriment caused by the colonial relationship with England. Moreover, he professed Home Rule as the pathway to getting the gentry to exercise a responsible role. Parnell even then linked self-government with economic development, a theme that was consonant with Butt's outlook but not universally shared by home rulers. His conception of self-government was positive; he believed that it brought out the best in men and civil society. To most Catholic nationalists self-government was the avenue to shaking off the domination of the Protestant Ascendancy. In 1874 the difference in purpose could be papered over; later, especially during the Land War and divorce crisis, the cracks imposed an intolerable strain. In spite of defeat (2,183 votes to 1,235) and modest display of talent, Parnell was quickly given a prominent place in League affairs. He had the exact qualities leaders of the Home Rule movement sought – his status as a Protestant landlord, the epitome of Ascendancy respectability. Additionally, Parnell was ready to dig into his own pocket in order to gain a place in the House of Commons.

At the public meeting of the Land Conference held in Dublin on 21 January 1875 Parnell called for legislation to give the tenant such security as would enable him to use resources to maximum effect. He wanted the tenant to possess the right of free sale of his holding, fair rent so long as proper agriculture was pursued and power to bequeath his property. An intriguing part of his short declamation was what amounted to a 'Celticist' interpretation: 'let them not forget that the basis of tenure [outside Ulster] . . . was of far older origin, and in its original and ancient integrity, many centuries back, gave equal claims to the tenant with those enjoyed by the North at a comparatively modern date'.[5] Linked to this, the following day at the Home Rule League meeting he insisted, 'if they were permitted to manage their own affairs they would attain all the prosperity the country required'.[6]

His political aspirations were untrammelled. When the County Tipperary representation fell vacant in early 1875, Parnell offered to contest the by-election against any Conservative. In the event, John Mitchel, a revered figure from the 1848 rebellion, stood – not to promote Home Rule but in opposition to it. Parnell ostentatiously contributed £25 towards Mitchel's expenses.

In April 1875 Parnell's opportunity came when the Home Rule League executive endorsed him for the Meath seat, vacant through the death of the Young Ireland veteran, John Martin. The League abrogated its policy of neutrality between competing Home Rulers and placed pressure upon a local candidate to withdraw. Parnell ensured his success by gaining the support of the local Catholic bishop, Thomas Nulty; the clergy acted as the chief election agents in his campaign. On 12 April at Navan, County Meath, he declared support for the principal demands of the Catholic elite – tenant right, denominational education and release of the remaining Fenian prisoners – seasoning his speech with a dash of insurrectionary rhetoric. Additionally, he was anything but bashful about claiming an inherited national consciousness.[7] Three features merit notice – his emphasis on the moral virtue of self-government; government for the people by the will of the people; and the pledge to employ all his energies in promoting the interests of everyone in the country. The first two embodied his conception of government and also of the corporate nature of nation.

HOME RULE: PARTY AND COUNTRY

Fifty-nine candidates professing Home Rule principles won sixty seats, including Philip Callan's double-return, at the general election held between 31 January and 12 February 1874; all but a handful met on 3 March 1874 and constituted an independent Irish party under the chairmanship of Isaac Butt. What sort of party was this? Edmund Burke's definition in 1770, stating that a 'party is a body of men united for promoting by their joint endeavours the national interest upon some particular principle in which they are all agreed' describes the core attributes of this new assemblage.[8] Focus on the Home Rule party, an organisation which was primarily a Westminster institution, is consonant with Weber's observation that at this stage of political development parties in the country simply do not exist in the 'form of permanent associations organised across local boundaries. Cohesion is provided solely by the members of Parliament.'[9] Quick results were expected by an aroused Irish public, but the mechanism of a modern party to promote its agenda was absent. Butt's personal standing with Fenians earned a grace period of three years for the parliamentary experiment. Conservatives captured 350 of 653 seats, giving them a secure majority and the prospect of governing for up to seven years. After an initial burst of enthusiasm, ingrained defects in the party surfaced. It was a fragile coalition, short of funds, lacking single-minded leadership, marred by the character of MPs who too often stayed away from Westminster, did not owe their election to the Home Rule League and with many lethargic about self-government. There were few signs of a carefully constructed strategy; political support for the movement at home was tenuous.

Butt had a realistic, possibly overly prosaic sense of the predicament. He appreciated that Irish success required time, an augmentation of party numbers at future elections, and that Home Rule influence rested on public opinion at home. Still, he anticipated that the Conservatives 'would offer them many things of material advantage to the country'.[10] The object of parliamentary representation in the current environment was, Butt said, to 'make themselves and their country respected. They would put forward their country's wrongs. They would demand their country's rights.' The House of Commons and the British public would have to be informed about Ireland. Butt 'did not at present ask the House to concede home rule to Ireland', for it 'remained to be discussed, and perhaps to be discussed for many years'.[11] His approach required patience, and it was also necessary for the new government to make visible concessions.

At the National Convention in November 1873 at which the Home Rule League was established, some delegates advocated

employment of obstruction in the House of Commons. Acknow-
ledging that this by no means new tactic was legitimate, Butt did
not think the moment was right for its deployment. In March 1874
the virtual organ of the movement, *The Nation*, threatened that
MPs might resort to 'making themselves troublesome at unexpected
times' if the ministry refused Irish demands.[12] Prior to Parnell's
election obstruction was already polarising opinion.

LEARNING THE ROPES

The years from 1875 to 1880 were decisive for Parnell's political
education. He advocated peasant land ownership as the solution to
the land question which would allow the upper classes to join
forces with the Catholic masses; self-government as the cement
holding disparate factions to the national agenda while also being a
mechanism for uniting Irish traditions; a belief in the innate virtue
of locally rooted elected government, because only laws made in
such institutions would be accepted by the governed; commitment
to progressive social and political ideas; and a desire to make Irish
representation and the House of Commons germane. Parnell
utilised and expanded upon forms of popular politics, especially
the use of enlarged literacy, allowing social and political communication at a distance. He bound together ideas in a fresh and
ordered package. Benedict Anderson sees new forms of communication as the key mechanism for welding physically disparate
people into real if 'imagined communities'.[13] Anderson observes
that ethnic communities were necessarily 'imagined' in the sense
of linking groups of people together who have not had and cannot
anticipate having direct physical acquaintance with one another.
This he insists only happens when modernisation reaches the
stage where print communication enables disparate peoples to
imagine a common bond. Bernadette Lally notes the role of

reading rooms, local newspapers and schools as the agents of print culture.[14] Perhaps no one more than Parnell in modern Ireland so underscores Anderson's hypothesis; his gifted exploitation of the press initiated an enterprising dimension of the national movement.

Obstruction intruded just as Parnell took his seat; though he did not participate, the new member noted the popular appeal of obstruction, instinctively understanding its importance. Throughout his subsequent public career he focused his energy on the House of Commons; public opinion was marshalled behind his parliamentary efforts. His record in parliamentary divisions [votes], debates, and question time shows someone who took the work seriously. At all points in his career he stressed the linkage between public opinion and parliamentarianism – Ireland's aspirations could only be gained when the two forces moved in tandem.

Parnell was not an instant success at Westminster but he quickly developed a sense of how parliamentary labour might be used, mirroring Walter Bagehot's *The English Constitution*. According to Bagehot, the House of Commons was the 'efficient' portion of the constitution, the cockpit of responsible government with five major functions: (1) to elect and sustain a ministry which he defined as its most important business; (2) to express the mind of the nation 'on all matters which come before it'; (3) to teach the country 'what it does not know'; (4) to inform the sovereign people of complaints and grievances which 'I am disposed to reckon . . . as the second function of Parliament in point of importance, that to some extent it makes us hear what otherwise we should not'; (5) to legislate.[15] Home Rulers could not make an equivalent impact on all of these. At various points Parnell gave differing emphases to each of Bagehot's functions. His techniques came to fruition at the time when the role of the House of Commons itself was in transition and the modernisation of political communications allowed new forms of popular politics to flourish. He was among the pioneers who adapted the endeavours of an elite assembly into something pertinent to the masses who were geographically and socially remote from London. There was always an underlying irony to Parnell's career. Although he developed into one of the towering figures of the House of Commons, his abiding aim was to remove himself from its precinct. The tensions inherent in Parnell's approach and the inconsistencies of his words resulted partly from the dilemma facing any person or group seeking concessions and interacting with a body it proposed to vacate.

On 26 April 1875 Parnell briefly attracted attention with a maiden speech criticising the government for failing to listen to the opinion of the Irish people.

> in the neglect of the principles of self-government lay the root of all Irish trouble. He trusted that the time would arrive when the history of the past would be forgotten, so far as it reminded England that she was not entitled to Ireland's confidence, and when she would give to Irishmen the rights which they claimed – the right of self-government – why should Ireland be treated as a geographical fragment of England, as he had heard an ex-Chancellor of the Exchequer call it some time ago. Ireland was not a geographical fragment, but a nation.[16]

Parnell's career-long theme stressed self-government as the bedrock of all Irish needs.

Parnell's parliamentary and public speeches in 1875, though still relatively unsophisticated in presentation, offered an insight into his ideas. Parnell spoke infrequently in the House of Commons during the remainder of his first session but he voted in 34 divisions, a commendable record, particularly in a party renowned for its laxity. His interventions in the House of Commons showed a populist mentality. In the instance of the alleged ill treatment of an imprisoned Fenian on 8 July Parnell stressed the crucial importance of forming and marshalling public opinion, telling the House of Commons: 'the Irish people objected to the treatment of the Irish political prisoners and he hoped that if Parliament did not take up the case English public opinion would be clearly expressed concerning it'.[17] There always remained an element of ambiguity in Parnell's attitude to English public opinion. At times he placed little faith in it, but at others, and more regularly, he thought it was a force for justice, if only it were properly informed.

Parnell's complaint about the education system is a typical case of a Home Ruler, particularly a Protestant, courting clerical support. Yet at the same time he made the key point that Westminster government was not sufficiently responsive, and that laws ought to be made by men who had the confidence of the governed. Legislation, he suggested, in order to be respected, had to be made in accord with public feeling. He reminded the House of Commons on 31 July that 'he did not believe that the system could be estimated by a comparison of the number of children that passed in reading and writing, nor the number that attended school'.[18] Whatever its secular accomplishments the system did not satisfy the religious susceptibilities of the majority of Irish people.

During the autumn of 1875 Parnell spoke five times in Ireland. These speeches received only limited notice, but in them he enunciated his standard themes, advocating that the best way to influence political opinion in Britain was by vigorous participation in the House of Commons. At an amnesty demonstration at Enniscorthy on 3 October, Parnell employed revolutionary imagery to press his view that the winning of national objects could only come when the people stood together in a determined way and did not depend on their representatives.[19] Parnell's instinctive trademark was to press a case with radical-sounding rhetoric accompanied by fairly moderate objectives. He discovered virtually from the beginning that both the Irish people and British critics heard the radical language not the measured ends. On 17 October at Nobber, Parnell defended the utility of representation and drew attention to his regular attendance at the House of Commons.[20] For Parnell parliamentary labour was meant to deliver boons and not serve only as a forum to make the case for Home Rule. He appreciated that the people of Ireland wanted concrete measures, articulating a formula – strict adherence to the grand principle of self-government while under this canopy other and sometimes contentious sectional claims could be advanced. Parnell emphasised the value of parliamentary representation, but warned that the people should monitor the activities of their MPs. He also made it clear that he was not an uncritical admirer of the eighteenth-century constitution which had become for many Home Rulers a national beacon. He rejected institutions that excluded any part of 'the nation'.

DEVELOPING A VOICE, 1876

The session of 1876 was crucial to Parnell's maturation. His stadium was the House of Commons where he spoke more regularly and voted in nearly one hundred divisions. He addressed a number of topics, learning to utilise procedural motions and Question Time. By the close of the session he was practised in parliamentary arts.

At a meeting of the Home Rule League in Dublin on 18 January Parnell urged the centrality of the self-government question, stressing as well the importance of both MPs and the Irish people acting with determination.[21] On 10 March he introduced a bill enabling Lessees' and Tenants' holding land under the Irish Church Temporalities Commissioners the right of purchasing the fee simple of their holdings.[22] The bill came to nothing but revealed him as an advocate of tenant land purchase. As early as 21 March he used non-Irish discussions to draw attention to Ireland's grievances. During discussion on 4 April of the adulteration of Irish whiskey with imports from Scotland, Parnell showed that he was developing parliamentary ingenuity. 'If the regulations of the Government were such as to render it necessary that good Irish whiskey should be mixed with the wretched Scotch stuff, and that the Irish people should be poisoned by it', Parnell postulated, 'then he thought that every Irishman, whatever might be his politics, would admit that the sooner they had their own Customs House under the control of an Irish Parliament, and their own Irish Chancellor of the Exchequer, the better.'[23] On 19 May he made what would become a standard complaint, objecting 'to the practice on the part of hon. Members who had not attended the discussion during the evening, but who came down to the House at a late hour and voted without knowing the merits of the question at issue'.[24] Parnell made a splash on 30 June when he responded provocatively to a reference by the Chief Secretary, Sir Michael Hicks Beach, to the killing of the van guard during the rescue of Fenians in 1867: 'The right hon. Gentleman looked at me so directly when he said he regretted that any Member of this House should apologise for murder, that I wish to say as publicly and as directly as I can that I do not believe, and never shall believe, that any murder was committed at Manchester.'[25] This display was reward with the applause of Fenians, showing Parnell's acute sense of the grand gesture and replicating his declamation the previous October. Yet the basis for his comment was the status of the law, not the absence of a felony.

At the beginning of July 1876 the *The Nation* called for a 'policy of obstruction' to show the government that 'the Irish meant business'.[26] Even the Irish Chief Secretary was alarmed: 'We have opposed nearly every bill or motion brought forward by private members, and passed no bill of our own of any real importance.'[27]

AFTER THE SESSION

Following three years of expressing popular feeling and informing
the House of Commons about Irish wants, only a Municipal
Corporations bill had passed. Irish opinion increasingly became
sceptical of Butt's teachings on the value of parliamentary representation. Parnell himself was not discouraged though he had
developed reservations concerning current usage. In the autumn
of 1876 he and John O'Connor Power, Home Rule MP for County
Mayo, travelled to the United States for the celebration of the
centenary of its revolution and to present an address from the Irish
people. On his return, speaking at Liverpool on 13 November to an
audience composed largely of Fenian sympathisers, Parnell stressed
the necessity of educating public opinion, 'they had another duty
to perform, which was to educate public opinion in England upon
Irish questions, which he looked upon as a difficult and almost
impossible task – so difficult that he had often been tempted to
think it was no use trying to educate English public opinion'. After
lauding the example of the militia he had just witnessed in New
York, Parnell reminded his hearers of the limited purposes a
similar body would have in Ireland.

> If in Ireland they could ever have under Home Rule such a national
> militia they would be able to protect the interests of Ireland as a nation,
> while they would never wish to trespass upon the integrity of the
> English empire, or to do harm to those they then would call their
> English brothers. It was a foolish want of confidence that prevented
> Englishmen and the English Government from trusting Ireland.
> They know Ireland is determined to be an armed nation, and they fear
> to see her so, for they remember how a section of the Irish people in
> 1782, with arms in their hands, wrung from England Legislative
> Independence. [28]

Parnell always insisted that in order to be a nation, Ireland must possess a militia.

Parnell, as yet, had not found a mechanism to secure a general public hearing. Between 1874 and the beginning of 1877 Parnell addressed audiences in Ireland fewer than twenty times and many of these occasions received slight journalistic notice. Indeed only three of these speeches took place during 1876 and merely one in the autumn, at Liverpool. The challenge then was to find ways of circumventing information blockage, resulting from the monopoly exercised by an indifferent press.

CHAPTER 3

Obstruction, 1877

COMMUNICATION AND MODERNISATION

James Bryce observes, 'Oratory is the usual avenue to leadership in a democratic movement, and Mr Parnell is one of the few who have arrived at a power neither by that road nor by military success. . . . So far from glittering with the florid rhetoric supposed to characterise Irish eloquence, his speeches were singularly plain, bare, and dry. Neither had they any humour.'[1] H. C. G. Matthew draws attention to the function of rhetoric in the later Victorian age when only two avenues of communication were then available – speeches and the printed word. Speeches, he points out, were 'not simply or even mainly declaimed to those present'.[2] Gaining attention in the press could quickly elevate a politician to public stature. A 'nationally integrated reporting system offered the means for a nationally integrated political rhetoric', Matthew maintains. His perceptive analysis of communication affords an appropriate framework for consideration of Parnell's exceptional and innovative use of the media. Parnell was catapulted into public esteem despite the fact that he controlled no machine, spent little money on politics, had no base in the countryside and exercised no patronage.

Six episodes proved crucial to Parnell's career; the first and in certain ways defining moment came in 1877 in the guise of the obstruction crisis. It turned Parnell into a national quasi-insurrectionary figure, albeit one steering a strictly constitutional course. At first glance it is a paradox that the imposition of a distinctly parliamentary tactic in a far-away chamber of an institution that Home Rulers vowed to exit moulded Parnell's reputation. Perhaps, though, it is less a paradox when the context and Parnell's own preferences are taken into account.

Microscopic investigation of 1877 brings to the fore:

- Parnell's intense focus on the House of Commons;
- His emergent skills as a parliamentarian and speaker;
- His role as a protest politician;
- Development of a personal political and constitutional ideology;
- His affinity with an English Liberal ethos;
- The extent to which Parnell and obstruction fit theoretical paradigms.

Obstruction revealed to Parnell a means of projecting himself and the Home Rule party to Ireland and the Irish abroad without the rigours and limitations of mass demonstrations. By 1877 there were vast changes, making globalised Irish politics a reality. Three-quarters of the population was literate in English and the remainder had access to political information by word of mouth, enjoying 'virtual literacy'. After mid-century there was rapid growth of periodicals, catering for the enlarged audience. Between 1849 and 1879 railway track expanded from 428 to 2,285 miles in Ireland with only remote hamlets remaining relatively inaccessible. This network allowed politicians to range widely and for a patriotic press in Dublin or other main centres to penetrate all corners of the island. Furthermore, the rail system was vital to the growth of an efficient postal system. Letters per head rose from 2.9 annually in the mid-1840s to 17.3 in the early 1880s. By then letters posted in London normally reached Cork within 24 hours. The telegraph transmitted material quickly and Parnell was a compulsive user of it. By 1880 more than 1.5 million telegrams were dispatched in Ireland. Preferential telegraph rates for newspapers under the Telegraph Act of 1868 meant that the deliberations of the House of Commons and public addresses by prominent politicians were the stable fare of a still mainly political press. The Atlantic had been transformed into an information highway. The main obstacle to politicians was not the speed of transmission but securing access to the means of communication. What increasingly distinguished Parnell was his manipulation of the unseen Irish polity.

BUTT AND PARNELL

Parnell came to differ with Butt on the weighting of the respective functions of representation. Significantly, neither man questioned participation in the business of the House of Commons. Many people in Ireland had little use for it, and not all of these were wild-eyed radicals. Butt and Parnell came to differ on how most effica-ciously to accomplish the Home Rulers' agenda. The dispute over obstruction saw Parnell expand his skills and sharpen his political ideology, articulating constitutional principles and ideals consonant with British Radicalism. Through his involvement he vociferously promoted tenant land purchase, and, even more crucially, he saw self-government principles not only as a panacea for Ireland but as the means by which various traditions could be woven together into a nation. His synthesis owed much to the earlier Protestant view of self-government. In addition, Parnell came to see that other Irish reforms were sectional, often divisive; Home Rule alone had a unifying effect. While neither reform nor Home Rule was effective standing singly, the appeal to self-government required primacy. If it was not a new formula, Parnell gave it a fresh twist. He routinely reverted to Home Rule as the means of warding off opponents, of forestalling divisions within the movement. This worked uneasily until December 1890 when others, mobilising what had been the bedrock of his constituency as well as exploiting the same networks of communication, cut the ground from beneath him.

Max Weber follows Michael Ostrogorski's *Democracy and the Organisation of Political Parties* (1902), tracing the formation of mass modern parties to the aftermath of the Second Reform Bill in 1867. A vastly enlarged electorate necessitated new modes of political organisation. Butt's party was formed shortly after the new conditions emerged; it would be unreasonable to expect Home Rulers to be on an identical plane to British parties, not least because franchise extension, a key aspect of the Ostrogorski/ Weber thesis, was much more restrictive in Ireland until enlargement of the electorate and elimination of small boroughs in 1884–5. Ostrogorski and Weber emphasise William Gladstone's role in the transformation; Parnell has a parallel place in Ireland. For Weber a key ingredient was the victory of the machine geared to the organisation of mass democracy over the older form of organisation that he termed parties of local notables.[3] The distinction between a dominant party machine and a party of local notables is of central importance. The Home Rulers were still at the stage of being a party of local notables. Weber additionally drew attention to 'new' politicians who lived 'for' and 'from' politics. Parliamentary stewardship was unpaid and scarcely a handful of Home Rulers derived meaningful financial returns from their political engagement. Moreover, only a small minority of Home Rulers lived 'for' politics, a number that, however, did include Butt himself along with most of the MPs who became 'obstructionists', perhaps above all Parnell. As Weber remarks, local notables and professional politicians conceive of, and execute, their parliamentary duties in different ways. Sigmund Neumann distinguishes between parties of individual representation and social integration.[4] The first joins together for elections, the second seeks to be the continuous and overarching focus of members' lives. Again over obstruction, the militant faction and traditionalists clashed on conceptions of party. In this framework the obstruction controversy was a struggle between Home Rulers who looked forward to a party that lived 'for' politics and those who clung to the traditional concept of a party of local notables. This was not simply young versus old, or militants against moderates, but it threw up the much more pertinent quest – the professionalisation of politics and the creation of a party of social integration.

An Irish party could not anticipate playing much part in the making and breaking of governments or from legislating except when they could co-operate with a British party or held the balance of power in the House of Commons, as Parnell partly did in 1885–6. Overly cordial collusion, however, held perils; identification with a ministry or British party tended to enervate the independence of Irish MPs, thereby undermining their standing with vital segments of opinion at home. It proved a long-term dilemma which Parnell uniquely evaded. Yet a national contingent could take full advantage of the expressive, teaching and informative functions. Between 1874 and 1876 Butt attempted to advance all three functions; Parnell during that time did not articulate an alternative vision, but he found a means to give the message a salience previous missing. Parnell's contribution was to insist that both the people of Ireland and her representatives ought to be in earnest. Thus Parnell's conception of representation was largely compatible with Butt's, but he stressed the importance of vigorous activity in Parliament and wanted greater fidelity to the principle of self-government. He realised that public opinion was frustrated. If parliamentary representation were to thrive, it had to be credible.

During 1877 Parnell emerged as an obstructionist and, significantly, a critic of Butt's leadership, though his transmutation occurred principally as a result of the old chieftain's refusal to swim in the shifting tide of opportunism. This is surprising, for Butt was an instinctual opportunist. Butt was advised to harness the force Parnell unleashed but he remained oblivious to this counsel. His obstinate refusal to bow to the cries for an active approach had several pragmatic reasons, stemming from a fear that frivolous protests would alienate members of his coalition and crucial British support. Instead he pleaded for 'the English Liberal to join us in demolishing every part of the system opposed to their principles . . . If we fail, we have supplied another, and an un-answerable argument to Europe, to the Irish and English nations, to show that nothing but self-legislation can ever reconcile us or realise our aspirations.'[5] Butt's cure was commendable, but it proved worse than the disease. However, ultimately, Butt stance was personal and, by taking it, he rather than Parnell proved to be the forcing house of obstruction.

'Obstruction' facilitated development of Parnell's speaking and parliamentary skills and revealed him to be knowledgeable – indeed he was a formidable parliamentarian in the making. Perhaps above all it revealed a man who held his own in the rough and tumble of the House of Commons.

OBSTRUCTION CONTROVERSY

Before the session began, many voices were calling for increased activity by the Irish members. It is doubtful that Parnell antici-pated a challenge to Butt or foresaw parliamentary activism as a pathway to his personal elevation. Indeed, as suggested already, it was a dispute that ought never to have happened and much of what transpired was the consequence of responses by Butt, the Conservative government, British MPs and the London press. The emergence of a systematic doctrine of 'obstruction' and the controversy over it is divisible into three stages – the period up to Whitsun when the main action took place in House of Commons and the public had only a sketchy insight into personal rivalries; late May to the close of August when the issue was pursued both in and out of Parliament; and the public contest between Butt and Parnell from the end of August until the national conference in January 1878.

The Queen's Speech at the opening of the new session offered little prospect of Ireland receiving boons. Initially, the obstructionist case was that Ireland was neglected and the only means to draw attention to this lacuna was by direct action in the House of Commons. Vigorous participation in debates on a range of topics and employment of procedural motions were the weapon to hand. Home Rulers initiated 15 bills, appropriating a large slice of private members' time. Parnell never intended his involvement to be essentially negative, though his critics could be forgiven for thinking otherwise. On 14 February Parnell gave a clear indication of support of land purchase in a debate on the Irish Church Act Amendment Bill: 'there was no doubt that the agricultural tenants were almost universally anxious to purchase their farms, and would do so if they had the means'.[6] He predicted that wider proprietorship 'would promote the prosperity, contentment, and independence of some 1,800 industrious heads of families in Ireland'.

Parnell defined his rationale for wide-ranging parliamentary involvement on 8 March: 'he did not intend to speak upon the subject of the Prisons Bill, but so long as he was an Irish Member, obliged to come to Parliament, sitting at Westminster, he would endeavour to take part in the discussions on all questions which might affect his country'.[7] With the assistance of a handful of other MPs, Parnell began routinely to use procedural motions to slow down government business; Parnell did not interfere in Private Members' time.

In his first public speech of the year given to the Liverpool Home Rule Association on 20 March, Parnell separated himself from the meeting chairman's criticism of the Home Rule MPs but he 'thought that they might show much greater earnestness'.[8] He was attempting to avoid a confrontation, not exasperate fractures within the party. On 26 March he answered the objections by the Chancellor of the Exchequer to 'repeated divisions on the part of such a small minority', declaring:

> It was incorrect in any hon. Member to say that he was chargeable with obstructing the business of the House. His opinion on that was that the action of obstruction should, when it was employed, be like that of the bayonet, short, sharp, and decisive. He would, however, never shrink from endeavouring to obtain a hearing for anyone who wished to raise a reasonable discussion.[9]

Later in the same debate he reasserted the constitutional principle, 'it was sometimes a duty to be in opposition to the House'. The young Irishman presented himself as an upholder of parliamentary privilege, a defender of minority rights, thereby establishing his credentials as a paragon of the Constitution. But to a mass Irish audience he personified protest and resistance.

Butt wrote privately to rebuke Biggar on 29 March. In this letter, not known to the public until published in the *Freeman's Journal* on 24 May, Butt alleged that obstruction alienated support, endangering issues of interest to Ireland, and undermined his leadership which had been conferred by the Irish people. His letter was a turning point. In the aftermath, the gulf between Parnell and his leader widened. On 12 April Butt's ire burst forth in the House of Commons: 'He must express his disapproval of the course taken by the hon. Member for Meath. It was a course of obstruction – and one against which he must enter his protest.'[10] Parnell responded on 14 April, again in a letter only published in late May, 'I must then, in future claim for myself that liberty of action upon Imperial and English matters which has hitherto been granted to every member of the party while I shall continue to follow your lead in regard to Irish questions.'[11] To this Butt replied on 21 April, 'unity on general questions would give us power and influence in the house'.[12]

Differences flared on 1 May when Parnell dissented from Butt on how to solve the land question. Butt stated 'that there was no great anxiety on the part of the Irish tenant occupiers to become the purchasers of their holdings'.[13] Parnell, though, rapidly ceasing to follow Butt's lead even on Irish questions, insisted, 'if a fair opportunity of purchasing their farms was presented to them they would embrace it with the utmost eagerness ... the question would never be settled on any other basis than that of giving to the Irish people the right and liberty of living on their own farms as owners.'[14] Support for an ultimate tenant ownership separated Parnell from most of his party and fellow landlords while bringing him closer to Fenian and radical agrarian outlooks.

PARLIAMENTARY AND PUBLIC CONTROVERSY

The controversy became fully public and bitter with Butt's publication of his correspondence with Biggar and Parnell. Until 21 August Parnell did not speak in Ireland; he justified his tactics to his British audience. Parnell found that his defence was not reported completely or accurately. Butt, when receiving the freedom of the city of Limerick on 22 May, said, 'I have felt it my duty to rebuke those who have endeavoured to sow dissension, and in showing dissention to break up the only political organisation that is at the present moment doing good for Ireland.'[15]

Parnell's letter published on 28 May set out the justification for parliamentary activism and accused Butt of having been delinquent in his leadership. He also argued that his participation actually increased support from English MPs. Crucially he attacked the laxity of the majority of Home Rule representatives, a theme that would receive emphasis in coming months.[16] That same day Parnell elaborated his position in Glasgow:

> He had believed that if the Irish members of Parliament would show that they were determined to obtain self-government – he did not mean local self-government, but national self-government – the people would be at their back, and give a support to the movement which would put it beyond failure . . . The policy which had directed the parliamentary action of the Home Rule party during the last four years had not obtained a single concession, save the barren one of the right of four or five Irish corporations to elect their own sheriffs. He thought the policy had condemned itself, and should be abandoned – and in its place a bolder policy adopted – a policy of hostility – and, if necessary, a policy of inconvenience to English interests – so long as she inconvenienced and injured their interests.[17]

On 5 June a party meeting attempted to find a bridge between Butt and the activists but this line in the sand immediately dissipated. Parnell on 11 June criticised Butt's ideas, not just his inactivity. He made three pertinent points: Ireland was inappropriately governed by unrepresentative boards; British policy had the effect of dividing the aristocracy from the people; and only locally rooted self-government could meet the country's needs satisfactorily. Observing not for the first time that 'there was no country in the world so much governed by Boards, and everybody who had lived in Ireland must have seen instances where the power of the Local Government Board and of the Commissioners of Public Works have been exercised adversely to the interests of the country'.[18] He then castigated the mistakes perpetrated by these bodies, insisting that the situation would not be remedied until local affairs were in the hands of people who commanded the confidence of the governed.

At Hatton Garden, London, on 19 June he developed four themes – MPs had not done their duty, Irish representation required remodelling, the Westminster atmosphere tended to corrupt, and the potential impact of men who stuck to their commitments.[19] At Liverpool on 14 July he repeated his core criticisms but added three further elements – too many MPs, English and Irish alike, treated Parliament as an embellishment to their social pretensions, the Home Rulers had not pursued a 'national' policy, and the Irish people should intervene in the interests of the 'nation'.[20] The importance Parnell attached to Irish opinion surfaced again on 23 July in the House of Commons, when he complained: 'This so called national system of education had been carried out without the slightest reference to Irish opinion on the subject.'[21]

During the South Africa bill debate on 25 July Parnell took exception to his treatment: 'deliberate intimidation has been resorted towards me by the Press of this country in order to coerce me, and to prevent me from doing what I consider my duty; and so long as I have the honour of a seat in this House I shall not allow myself to be prevented from speaking when I may think it necessary to speak, or from taking such steps as I may think necessary'.[22] Butt was losing control of the party and his influence in the country was on the wane. Once more he threatened resignation of the chairmanship on 27 July. Parnell's remarks on 28 July that the India Civil Service was a source of employment for the English middle-classes displayed his Radical propensities: 'They all knew that the Indian Civil Service was a very extensive one, and that a large number of the youth of the English middle classes found employment in it who could not otherwise find a field for their energy.'[23] This orientation was reaffirmed on 30 July during discussion of the South Africa bill: 'If the people were fit for Constitutional Government, their own wishes ought to have been consulted; and, if not, he could not think them in that case fit for confederation.'[24]

Even in the heady atmosphere of notoriety, Parnell remained sensitive to the charge of deliberate obstruction. On 27 July, in a letter to *The Times* published three days later, Parnell stressed his contribution to debates in the House of Commons, especially on the South Africa and prison bills. Furthermore, he suggested that hostility to his course was motivated by a refusal to recognise the legitimacy of Irish participation in British and imperial discussions. Parnell defended his actions on constitutional grounds: 'Believing it my right, as a member of the Imperial Parliament to take a part in all the business of the House, I have exercised it in spite of threats conveyed by letters and otherwise. I have pressed my views on various questions earnestly . . . and not with the dubious deference expected from an Irish member.'[25] He viewed himself as empowered to speak and act on all questions before the British nation. On 6 August the party sought to reach a compromise but this quickly evaporated. In a letter to *The Times* on 8 August, Parnell denied obstructionist intentions, again pointing to his role in improving bills.[26] During the session he voted in more than 200 of the 313 divisions.

Initially, Biggar and Parnell had been treated as a pair, but soon the focus was on Parnell. Although just one of a small set of so-called Irish 'obstructives', the press and people in Ireland identified the tactic and 'resistance' to British domination with Parnell. By sometimes blatant use of 'obstruction' and the forum of Westminster he was able to side-step the clergy and respectable elements in Ireland, obviating the need for an organisation or a public relations apparatus. Parnell had seen that only by appearing aggressive and committed could morale on the Irish benches and at home be restored.

PUBLIC DEFENCE OF THE ACTIVE POLICY
21 AUGUST–13 JANUARY 1878

It was clear that Parnell was gaining a spirited following. On 21 August the obstructive approach was upheld at a meeting in the Rotunda in Dublin and then on 27 August 1877, at a sparsely attended convention, Parnell in succession to Butt was elected President of the Home Rule Confederation of Great Britain. The Confederation had little importance but Parnell's ascendance was significant symbolically. At this juncture Parnell did not grasp fully the innovative feature of his approach – that he could affect a large but almost entirely unseen audience. He, in part, was wedded to the traditional and demanding role of public speaking and demonstrations. In reality he had few options as his efforts on the platform continued to receive a limited though expanding coverage. In September he and John O'Connor Power made a tour of northern English and west of Scotland towns and several venues in Ireland to publicise the policy of parliamentary activism. Parnell spoke in nine different places in Great Britain, usually to enthusiastic assemblages of receptive Irishmen who knew him by the reputation amassed through the press. His speeches were reproduced verbatim in local newspapers and by traditional norms the tour was successful, but Parnell's reach to an outside audience was constrained. The national press in London tended to allocate only brief references to his appearances and even Irish newspapers gave the tour limited coverage. Public speeches, like parliamentary participation, could only transcend the narrow confines of an immediate audience when these were published in prominent newspapers. Parnell's efforts did not suggest that he was on the threshold of an innovatory form of political communication.

As summer waned, Butt was greeted by a stream of well-wishers' advice on handling obstruction. Emmet Larkin suggests that Butt mounted an effective counter-attack, garnering support from the Irish bishops, who had little sympathy for Parnell's brand of politics.[27] Butt also commanded continuing affection amongst Fenians. According to Larkin, from mid-September Butt's strategy enforced moderation on Parnell. This is not borne out by Parnell's speeches, but it is true that he realised that the dispute had to be waged within parameters. In Belfast on 26 September he stated 'what is the only way they can prevent us from doing as we have done last session . . . There are two remedies – first, they can disfranchise the Irish constituencies and govern the country by martial law, or they can give us back the right of governing ourselves.'[28] He maintained that the abolition of tithes, and the Church and land acts 'were gained by exceptional means and methods. I say if Ireland wants to gain anything it is useless for her to rely upon ordinary parliamentary means or methods.' At a banquet in his honour the following evening he observed that he had spoken about 24 times on obstruction during the previous month. He pointed out that it was 'not a policy of obstruction at all; it was really a policy of independent and strenuous opposition to the government of the day all along the line in detail upon every question.'[29]

On 9 October at a party meeting facing sceptical colleagues, Parnell stuck to his guns, declaring: 'I think the course the Irish party have adopted in the past has not been calculated to attract the attention of the Irish people and to make them believe in our earnestness, and if we want them to support a parliamentary party we must show them that we are in earnest, and that we are determined to carry out that policy.'[30] He was of course speaking primarily for the unseen, not the present assemblage. Two days later the Home Rule League agreed to a conference to consider the active policy. As might be anticipated, the outcome of the conference hinged on the selection of delegates; Butt and the old guard ensured that they, not Parnell, would prevail. On 8 December Parnell staked out his position at Castlebar, County Mayo, in his first sojourn to the west. This speech had three important features. It adumbrates his comments at Cork city on 21 January 1885 enshrined on the Parnell monument in Dublin; he pointedly exploited the self-government aspiration and patriotic platitudes to quell internal divisions in national ranks; and once more he advocated peasant proprietorship as the ultimate solution to the land question.[31]

Bew notes that Parnell came away from his visit understanding that for western smallholders the land question was not simply one of rentals but the need for more land or reclamation of the waste lands.[32] In the 1880s he would sponsor an attempt to reclaim such land.

CONCLUSION

By 1877 Parnell judged that public opinion in Ireland could only be persuaded to continue supporting parliamentarianism if MPs acted in earnest. For him that necessitated greater emphasis on the expressive function and notably a resort to protest politics. In the course of the dispute Parnell learned how to make events at Westminster germane and exciting to the Irish people through the medium of the press. Parnell's use of the media essentially confirms Benedict Anderson's emphasis on communication as the key to forging identity amongst otherwise disparate populations. From 1877 Parnell effectively exploited the House of Commons to teach

Irish opinion the value of work at Westminster and in doing so moulded an Irish identity that had new and unifying character-istics and a corporate ethos. His method certainly transgressed on the susceptibilities of an English audience; he was doing what had never happened before under the Union, making the mundane intricacies of Westminster relevant to ordinary Irish people and most especially to Catholics who harboured suspicions about the utility of a Protestant, English and landlord-dominated assembly in London. Ironically, Irish opinion was enlisted for the active parliamentary approach by discussing British and imperial ques-tions. His undeniable achievement, though, was to focus attention and hopes on the House of Commons.

CHAPTER 4

Activism and the Dawn of the Land Question,
13 January 1878 to 7 June 1879

THE YEAR 1878

The active approach remained vibrant during 1878 and 1879; Parnell became more polished and adept at its implementation. It differed from the previous year in five respects:

- Greater skill allowed him to continue the active policy but be less blatant in his tactics;
- He developed from being primarily a protest politician into an agenda setter;
- He emerged more distinctively as a Radical reformer;
- He became increasingly critical of the political ideas of traditional Home Rulers;
- He articulated a more developed colonial or post-colonial interpretation of Ireland's ills.

There was no attempt until late in 1878 to conduct a public speaking campaign. During 1878 Parnell's public speeches numbered a mere ten, with the four in Ireland taking place between 21 October and 16 November. Whereas in 1877 activism was seen as something of a group effort with Parnell its most high-profile practitioner, thereafter he was clearly the leading proponent.

There was no diminution of his parliamentary efforts. He participated in at least 160 of 278 divisions.

Speaking at the national conference on 14 January, Parnell, realising his comparative isolation, was conciliatory though none-theless eager to stress the crucial role of continuous parliamentary participation. Yet a year later he lamented that the real issue had been placed on a back burner as a pre-conference agreement precluded open discussion of parliamentary tactics. Nevertheless, he assured the delegates that 'I will promise Mr Butt and the Government (and I think I can promise for the other "obstructive" members as well as myself) that if combined together they can succeed in giving us enough to do in bringing about beneficial legislation for Ireland during the next session, we will not attempt to interfere with any of these English bills.'[1]

On 18 January Parnell defined the active position to the House of Commons; it affords a major insight into his political ideology:

> if they thoroughly understood the vital importance of having the Land Question settled in such a way as to enable the soil of Ireland to produce the proper amount of food that it was capable of producing – if they could realise the position of a people without any University education that they could accept conscientiously – they would see that after all they were not so unreasonable in preferring the interests of their own countrymen to the interests of the people of England ...[2]

Moreover, he endorsed the widely accepted dogma that direct action had a role in achieving Irish objectives. In this he anticipated the strategy of the Land War. 'Home Rulers had got a programme ... They had a wide and varied platform ... They were in possession of these pressing questions, and they felt themselves entitled to bring them before the notice of the House at any and every convenient opportunity', he stated.

On 28 February his adherence to 'country principles' could be seen again in the debate on the Grand Jury Law Amendment (Ireland) Bill: 'Then they would have a greater feeling of responsibility as regarded the management of county affairs. When the barriers, separating class from class, were removed...the principle of representation might fairly be extended, and the ratepayers could have a more direct control over county management.'[3] In the debate on the Factories and Workshops Bill on 1 March Parnell took a Radical stance, declaring his support for protection of the workforce: 'Where the employment was unhealthy and the hours long, surely there was reason for protecting the persons employed in it, if protection were necessary in any case.'[4] Parnell again sported Radical credentials on 26 March in discussion of the Mutiny Bill when he also affirmed, 'a very slight acquaintance with history would convince anybody that reforms had always been due, in the first place, to the persistence and courage of a minority'.[5]

Parnell's views on the taxation of Ireland were ventilated on 4 April when he complained that 'successive Chancellors of the Exchequer had so framed their Budgets as that the largest part of the money taken from Ireland and Scotland for Imperial purposes was drawn from the very poorest of the people, instead of from the middle and upper classes, as was the case in England'.[6] To this he added, on 5 April, that 'tax should fall upon champagne, claret, or some other of those wines which were consumed by the upper classes as luxuries'.[7] He returned to taxation on 16 April, asserting, 'taxpaying power of Ireland was one-seventeenth of that of Great Britain; but, when he came to the contributions to the Imperial Revenue, he found that Ireland contributed one-eighth of that of Great Britain, or twice as much as she ought to pay'.[8]

The land question once more attracted his notice on 9 May; he restated support for allowing tenants to become owners of their holdings, demanding of the Irish Church Temporalities Commissioners 'that every facility should be given to the occupying tenants to become proprietors of these holdings, in order that it might be seen how far the creation of a small class of peasant proprietors would be attended with beneficial results'.[9] Parnell 'did not think there was any special way of settling the Irish Land Question. There were a great many ways; but the sale of lands to tenants was not an unimportant branch of the settlement. In Ireland, as elsewhere, there existed the natural desire on the part of a man to own the soil which he lived on'. Also, the same day, he decried the large difference in salaries civil servants in Scotland and Ireland received compared to those in England: 'This was part of a system, which he was sorry to see was very much practised in the preparation of these accounts, of starving the Civil servants in Ireland. In no cases were they given equivalent salaries to those in England.'[10]

Parnell reflected on the mechanisms of the House of Commons on 30 May, suggesting that the estimates should be examined by a small committee prior to being considered in the full House of Commons.[11] 'As an Irish Member, he felt great interest in the establishment of county government in England', he reaffirmed on 14 June.[12] 'Such might seem an extraordinary statement; but, as a matter of fact, if England suffered from the imperfection of its county government, Ireland suffered ten times as much. Both sides of the House agreed in the necessity of improvement in England; how much more desirable, then, must it be in Ireland?'

The Intermediate Education Bill was introduced in the House of Lords on 21 June and enacted on 6 August. By mid-1878 relations between Butt and Parnell reached a nadir; each sought to claim the education legislation for his own tactics. Parnell proved the more successful in the contest for public opinion, demonstrating that he knew when, where and how to strike. On 21

October the Home Rule Confederation of Great Britain re-elected Parnell President. He told the conference that the practice of activism forced the British Parliament to give 'the last two months of the session all to ourselves for Ireland. That was a thing they never did before, but I venture to predict that they will do it again.'[13] At Ballinasloe, County Galway, on 3 November Parnell claimed for the active policy the successes of the education legislation and release of political prisoners declaring, 'if half a dozen men could obtain these things by being energetic and determined, and representing the spirit that existed among the people of this country, and could fearlessly claim that if they returned to Parliament 25 or 30 active men . . . greater and better results would be obtained'.[14] He favoured tenants becoming owner-occupiers eventually but 'in the meantime, they must stop eviction, they must keep the people in the country, and prevent landlords from raising the rents.' At Tralee, in an impromptu address on 15 November, Parnell referred to the Intermediate Education Act 'as an example of what determination could do on wider fields, especially if they had a larger number of represen-tatives to exhibit it'.[15] In a major address at the Kerry Tenants Defence Association on 16 November, Parnell once more distin-guished between the longer-term ideal of tenant ownership and the present possibility for winning security of tenure. Because converting the tenants into owners could not happen immediately, he supported tenant right as the immediate object. On the issue of parliamentary activity he declared that in the face of a hostile Conservative government Irish members had an obligation to take resolute action for 'if their members felt all this in their hearts and showed it in season and out of season in the House of Commons upon any Irish question – he did not care whether it was the land question or the question of self-government – they were bound to win'.[16] Moreover he insisted there was no antagonism between land reform and home rule: 'he believed in self-government for Ireland, and he believed that every blow they struck for tenant-right, or for any other good Irish question, was a powerful stroke for self-government – he did not care which came first'.

Parnell's successes should not be overestimated, not least because neither he nor the wider public knew that Butt's influence was about to be cut short by the grim reaper. By 1879 Parnell had achieved notoriety mainly by espousing a sectional point of view and concentrating energy disproportionately on topics of marginal concern to people at home. He gained notice but lacked a galvanising issue and already obstruction seemed a limited piece of weaponry, perhaps exceeding its sell-by date.

JANUARY–7 JUNE 1879

In January 1879 in Sunderland, Durham and Newcastle, Parnell articulated the forward policy. At Sunderland on 13 January he laid out his theme on parliamentary activism and how it affected the Irish in Britain and ways in which they might aid the cause. 'The position of the Irish people in England was a very peculiar and a very powerful one. It would be but a truism to tell them they held the balance of power of parties in the town of Sunderland . . . he asked them to hold themselves in reserve, and to tell their mind to no man until the time came for action, and when that time came to make up their minds how to act, and to act together in a body.'[17] He claimed for activism the achievements that had been gained: 'A few of them had sought to impress these Irish questions on the Government and they had been successful so far – such for instance as the question of Intermediate Education.' John Ferguson, the influential Glaswegian, followed advocating the Radical nostrum of free trade in land; to its absence he attributed the current depression. In response Parnell reflected a Utilitarian philosophy, saying 'the land system both in England and Ireland was based upon false and bad principles, that the soil could not be cultivated in order to carry out the greatest good to the greatest number'.

In Durham the next evening he reiterated his message. He thought 'that the people might be enabled, if they returned a good honest Irish representation to the House of Commons, to do some good for their country. But he confessed that unless the Irish representation was considerably augmented, he saw no use at all in bringing about a balance of power. The majority of the present Irish members had not tried to do any good.'[18] At Newcastle on the 16th, in a more carefully prepared speech, he restated 'country' principles:

> The House of Commons was an impossible institution – nay, more, it was a mischievous and evil institution. It was mischievous to the people of this country, every liberty had been gained, not by the help of the House of Commons, but in spite of it. . . . He was thoroughly convinced that until you broke up the governing functions of the House of Commons, and distributed these functions among other legislative assemblies, they would never get a House of Commons in any part of the country that would govern for the advantage and according to the will of the people of England.[19]

The meeting of the Home Rule League in Dublin on 4 February was acrimonious. The old chieftain made his last appearance before it was subjected to an attack from John Dillon, while Parnell commented on Butt's declining health and looked beyond the current time to when the ailing leader would no longer be present. Again he declared the need for Irish members to be aggressive and insisted that activism rather than Butt's approach had forced the government to consider Irish wants. He proclaimed, 'I want them to take a practical and daily interest in the general business of the

House of Commons. I don't want anything more. I don't want them to obstruct, or tramp through the division lobbies all night.'[20] He accused Butt of initiating the controversy by writing and publishing letters. 'But as long as any Government, whether Conservative or Liberal, shows that it is mindful of the rights of our country by giving a reasonable portion of time of the session to the settlement of some leading Irish question, then I see no reason why we should be unfriendly or hostile to them.' Continuing, he said,

> I do not believe at all in refusing concessions. I am for a policy of taking what we can get and look for more afterwards. I do not believe that a settlement of the land question would injure the cause of self-government. If you have the Land Question settled on a permanent basis you remove the great reason that now exists in this country to prevent the very large, rich, and influential class of Irish landlords from falling in with the demand for self-government.

Ireland's sad circumstances, he implied, stemmed from the colonial relationship. Parnell professed to be happy for Butt to receive credit for accomplishments; he only wanted to secure results.

His theme was repeated at St Mary's Hall, Belfast on 10 February.[21] In the House of Commons on the 13th Parnell responded to the ministerial statement: 'It was now almost a matter of history with the Irish Party that concessions were not to be won from any English Government by a policy of conciliation.'[22] On 7 March he displayed his progressive credentials on the question of admitting women to the parliamentary franchise.[23] At Kilnaleck County Cavan on 14 April he reverted to the agrarian issue, defining 'the final settlement of the land question was the settlement which obtained in France and Belgium, where the farmer who worked the soil owned it.'[24] Addressing the Central Tenants' Association in Dublin on 16 April he proposed assisting the claims of English as well as Irish tenant farmers though believing that the relative situations of the two differed and the remedies would differ as well.[25] On 27 May he warned the House of Commons that the agricultural crisis had become grave. He demanded that something meaningful had to be done by the government or 'the question was one which would have to be taken up by the Irish Members in a firm and determined fashion', for the situation 'deeply affected their constituencies; and even if they were disposed to hang back a little on the subject, the constituencies would not allow them'.[26]

CONCLUSION

After 1878 Butt never returned to the House of Commons; he died on 5 May 1879. As a counter-factual historical exercise, it is interesting to ask what would have been Parnell's status had Butt's physical demise and the western agricultural crisis not intruded. Obstruction had proved a limited, if useful, tactic. However, Butt did die and there was a land war. Parnell's weakness was apparent in the by-election for County Cork, a constituency dominated by large farmers, held in mid-February. Moreover, he remained a pariah to many colleagues who mistrusted him and held the young MP responsible for Butt's decline. His stand on numerous questions won admiration from British Radicals. Even critics of his techniques could not deny that he was well informed on a range of issues and made the necessary effort to learn procedural forms, while also mounting a stern defence of minority rights.

CHAPTER 5

The Land War
8 June 1879–2 May 1882

INTRODUCTION

The Land War reshaped and mobilised nationalism, animated the Home Rule demand, provided the platform for reforming land holding, confirmed and created the essential myths of the nation and afforded the cultural environment that allowed Parnell to sweep all before him. It was a moment in time when nationalism was fused into a combustible compound. Yet if the Land War, with its demonstrations, intimidation and violence, seems at first glance the antithesis of constitutional principles, closer inspection of Parnell's part reveals just the opposite. Parnell, who often trailed rather than set the pace of the agitation, was able to place himself at its head, gaining credit for the accomplishment of an unprecedented Catholic unity and passage of important land legislation, thereby connecting the elusive moral and material strands of the national movement. In the course of the struggle Parnell's followers erected a 'royal' persona for him – with its cluster of associations evoking authority, deference and allegiance – as a significant element of the process of de-legitimising the authority of the British state in Ireland and at the same time advancing the interests of the nationalist movement.[1] Chief aspects were

- Further incremental elevation of Parnell's status;
- Effective command for a sufficient sector of the press to ensure favourable public exposure;
- An increased grip on the electorate to give him leadership of the parliamentary party;
- A central place in the British political process;
- First effective linkage of popular and parliamentary strands of nationalism;
- Effective exclusion of the Ascendency from the 'nation'.

Even as Butt was mourned, a sea change in Irish life loomed on the horizon. As a consequence of several poor harvests, many western tenants faced severe hardship. The Home Rule movement, though sympathetic to moderate land reform, was not an agrarian organisation. Parnell had identified himself with the demand for a peasant ownership as the ultimate solution, though supporting the demand for security of tenure and regulation of rentals immediately.

THE LAND AGITATION BEGINS

On 1 June 1879 Parnell met the prominent Fenian, John Devoy, who lived in America. Devoy had sent Parnell a telegram the previous October, offering him Fenian support. Parnell did not respond then but met Devoy and the revered Fenian John O'Leary in early March, and subsequently Devoy and Davitt in April prior to the Irishtown demonstration which Parnell did not attend and is usually held to mark the beginning of the Land War. According to Devoy, the outcome of the June 1879 meeting was that Parnell accepted what is known as the 'New Departure', a scheme meant to restore the co-operation that Butt had secured in 1874 between the advanced men and the parliamentarians. Whether Parnell acceded to the pact is in doubt; however, it contained nothing inimical to his outlook. This understanding proposed that: (1) the open movement should not be detrimental to the interests of Fenianism or its secret preparations for armed rebellion; (2) the demand for self-government, though not publicly defined for the present, must nevertheless be nothing short of a national parliament with full control over all matters of vital Irish interest, and include a responsible Irish executive; (3) a peasant proprietorship through compulsory land purchase should be defined as the solution to the land question; (4) Home Rule MPs should form an absolutely independent party.

On 8 June Parnell spoke at an agrarian demonstration in Westport, County Mayo. His involvement attracted considerable interest, but his actual remarks were once again restrained. Though supporting a peasant proprietorship, Parnell said the present aim was 'fair rent', defined as what 'the tenant can reasonably pay according to the times'.[2] He proceeded to caution tenants not to depend upon the members of Parliament. They must look only to themselves. Tenants, he stated, should 'show the landlords that you intend to hold a firm grip on your homesteads and land'. He did not attempt to tell the tenants how to go about defending themselves; he made no promise to guide their efforts personally. In the following weeks Parnell steered clear of the growing agrarian agitation while continuing to throw his energy into House of Commons business. He was present during the session for more than half of the divisions.

The National Land League of Mayo was formed on 16 August, giving the land campaign a focus; Parnell essayed the possibilities before speaking in Ireland on the last day of the month. He rapidly associated himself with the agitation and in the eyes of the world was identified as its foremost spokesman. His speeches during the autumn emphasised eight themes: tenants needed to stand together and help themselves; in the first instance tenants should seek rent abatements from landlords; the agitation should be conducted within the law; public opinion could be wielded to gain a resolution, in particular to secure government intervention to set fair rents; tenant ownership in the longer term was essential to build a prosperous country; the decline in the value of agricultural output was not short term but linked to the rise of American competition; town and country were connected intimately and everyone had an interest in the struggle; and only when Ireland had self-government would the needs of the people be met satisfactorily. Parnell, perhaps more than any of the other principal figures in the Land War, grasped its vicissitudes. For the vast majority of those who joined the campaign the issue was simpler and largely came down to a sectarian divide between landlord and tenant and, dangerously, Protestant and Catholic in the southern provinces. The 'nation' and Catholics became virtually synonymous.

When Parnell spoke at Limerick on 1 September he pointed to the successes of active participation in the House of Commons, omitting reference to the land question.[3] His next address on 11 September at the Home Rule League Convention again did not mention the land.[4] He proceeded to speak widely, mainly about land, addressing audiences in Ireland on more occasions than in any previous year. On 22 September at Tipperary, Parnell asserted that 'the land of this country cannot be cultivated unless the people of this country own it'.[5] It had long been his opinion that the land system was the cause of inefficient output and inadequate modernisation. His analysis can be compared to Barbara Solow's modern contention that under-renting of land was the true reason for the lag in output.[6] While encouraging organisation and self-help, Parnell said 'I should be sorry to encourage you to be determined unless I thought that you would gain a great benefit by it yourselves and for the whole country . . . Bring public opinion to bear upon the landlords, exert every force of passive resistance of wrongful eviction, and you must win.' Shortly afterwards, on 28 September, at Tullow, County Carlow, he repeated his own preference for tenant proprietorship but called for the government to establish a tribunal to set fair rents.[7] The next day he and Davitt jointly issued an 'Appeal to the Irish Race', seeking the aid of the diaspora for the agitation. Yet his advice to the tenants fell on the side of studied moderation. At a demonstration in Meath on 12 October he urged tenants to join together to meet the landlord and offer him a fair rent based on what they could afford.[8] He told an audience in Belfast on 15 October, an appropriate place to describe the joint interest of town and country, that the land question was an urban as well as rural necessity; the whole of Ireland was linked into one community on the issue.[9] Three days later he insisted,

Providence has placed in our hands a means of settling this great land question in Ireland. Our people are in Ireland today; they are determined to do what they can for themselves. I believe that by standing together, and by adopting a determined attitude – if you like, obstruction – towards the landlords, you will compel a solution to the great land question in the only way that such a question can be solved in Ireland. We cannot hope to obtain a settlement of any Irish question by means of ordinary action upon English public opinion, but we stand in a very strong and a very exceptional position. I hope, then, that the people of the town will unite with the people of the country, and, seeing that the interests of all classes are bound up in the solution of this great question, that there will be no rivalry between the town and country – but that they will stand together – that the shopkeeper will help the farmer and the farmer the shopkeeper, and that the man of business will see that his interests are connected in obtaining the abolition of this unjust and unnatural system. And if we can – taking advantage of this extraordinary opportunity – unite all classes in

Ireland in this way to aid in this scheme for land reform, I believe we will have done that which no Irishman ever had such an opportunity of doing before, and that we shall take one great step towards obtaining for our country the inestimable blessing of self-government by fixing upon the soil of Ireland those who cultivate that soil.[10]

Parnell's vision of unity, collective action and utilising the loco-motive power of the land question to promote self-government was not an innovation but certainly stood as a benchmark for the movement that was about to the grip the country. The irony, of course, is that the land campaign put paid to any pretensions of cross-religious or class collaboration except on terms set down by an ultra-Catholic wing of the national force.

On 21 October 1879 the Irish National Land League was established, with Parnell as President. He was now the recognised, if titular, leader of a land campaign driven in the main by local initiative. On 17 November in Roscommon he reiterated the advice he had given at Meath a month earlier, also supporting the principle of a peasant proprietorship:

We have laid down the principle that the land of Ireland ought to belong to the people of Ireland so we are also prepared to show you how that principle can be practically carried out. We don't urge the immediate adoption of our settlement of the question. We are willing to work with everybody who puts his shoulder to the wheel and tries to assist the people of this country.[11]

Following the arrest of some Land League leaders and the suspension of Michael Davitt's ticket-of-leave, he spoke at Balla, County Mayo, on 23 November urging that people act within the law:

I congratulate you upon your attitude today – calm, determined, self-reliant, and within the law. In this way we shall teach our rulers that although they may violate the Constitution, although they may rush into illegal acts, we are not going to be induced to follow them . . . You have shown that in keeping a firm grip of your homesteads, and in refusing to pay an unjust rent you have shown that advice is your only safety. But I would exhort you with all the little power or force that I may possess to maintain the attitude that you have maintained up to the present, and not to allow any provocation to draw you away from your duty. Even if your leaders are torn from your midst, let them go – others will take their places . . . [12]

NORTH AMERICAN TOUR

He agreed to visit North America in order to solicit contributions, sailing in the company of John Dillon to the New World on 21 December. This mission proved an outstanding success, securing more than £70,000 and elevating Parnell beyond that of mere leader of a sectional agitation into that of 'the uncrowned king of Ireland', a title bestowed by the rising journalist-politician T. M. Healy in Montreal near the close of the tour. It was the second of the key moments or incidents that shaped his career. Parnell had discovered, if by accident, during the obstruction struggle that he reached a wide audience not physically present through the press. The coverage of the North American mission confirmed and extended this mode of political communication, forming Parnell into an innovative and different type of leader. The autumn land meetings had been conducted along traditional lines and certainly during the tour he spoke to live gatherings, but the impact exerted was principally on a reading public far away.

On arrival in New York on 2 January 1880, Parnell saw the object of his undertaking only partly in terms of the land struggle;

he also wanted to inform Americans on the policy of parliamentary activism.[13] The shift of emphasis towards agrarian agitation, signalled at Madison Square Garden on 4 January and in Fall River, Massachusetts, on the 14th, came because of the deteriorating conditions in Ireland:

> We have changed somewhat from the original object for which we came to this country. Originally we came to this country for the purpose of enlisting your sympathy and support solely in behalf of our political movements in Ireland; but the immensity of the famine, and the certainty that unless something is done very speedily, in six or seven of the large counties in the West of Ireland, thousands will perish of the most horrible of all deaths, famine; so we have changed in obedience to the dictates of humanity and ask you to assist us in endeavouring to remove the distress in Ireland.[14]

The political purpose of the trip received less attention, but Parnell never abandoned it. From the outset he pointed out that the object of the Land League was to influence opinion in order to force the British government to reform the agrarian system. His most important address was to the United States House of Representatives on 2 February. Parnell's carefully prepared comments emphasised his and the 'national' prescription for amelioration of Ireland's poverty:

> The present famine, as all other famines in Ireland, has been the direct result of the system of land tenure which is maintained there. And while we have been compelled by the frightful condition of our people to appear before the American people in the guise of beggars, and to use every exertion to collect money to save life, I feel it to be equally my duty to point out to you the cause which keeps Ireland in a condition of chronic poverty and brings on from time to time such horrible famines

as that which is at present raging there. When the task is thrown upon America of feeding a people who have been driven into starvation by ruinous and unjust laws, surely you acquire a right to express your opinion very freely on the character of those laws and on the policy of maintaining them. And I have every confidence that the public sentiment of America will be a great assistance to our people in their present effort to obtain a just and suitable settlement of the Irish land question. Since I have been in this country I have seen so many tokens of the good wishes of the American people toward Ireland that I feel entirely at a loss to express my sense of all the enormous advantage and service which is being daily done in this way to our cause. I do not seek to embroil your Government with the government of England; but we claim that the public opinion and sentiment of a free country like America is entitled to find expression wherever it is seen that the laws of freedom are not observed.[15]

His intention was to influence American opinion, thereby putting pressure on the British government to legislate.

The mission was organised by the revolutionary Clan na Gael, though Parnell later would deny its role. Not surprisingly, Parnell tried to flatter the prejudices of his hosts. He affirmed the self-government objective, usually towards the close of each speech, and sometimes uttered radical-sounding phrases. At Cincinnati on 20 February he allegedly said:

And let us not forget that that is the ultimate goal at which all we Irishmen aim. None of us – whether we are in America or in Ireland; or wherever we may be – will be satisfied until we have destroyed the last link which keeps Ireland bound to England.[16]

Whether he actually used the words 'until we have destroyed the last link' is uncertain (newspaper accounts of the speech are not consistent), but he did make similar comments elsewhere during the tour. The core of his message, however, emphasised the legal and constitutional purposes of the Land League. To the person who called out at Peoria, Illinois, on 2 March that landlords should be shot, Parnell made the counter-proposal, foreshadowing his speech at Ennis on 19 September 1880:

> It is one of the principles of the English Constitution that when anyone has any grievances against the crown, he is not bound to contribute to its support. We will apply the same principle to the landlords and cut off their supplies. By so doing we will make the landlords think it is to their interest as much as the tenants to have the question settled.[17]

Parnell had the particular gift of divining when to use a dramatic gesture, the *bon mot*, in order to enlist support for non-violent remedies. But the essence of his message was to fasten attention on the resolution of grievances within the framework of the Westminster Parliament.

GENERAL ELECTION AND ELECTION AS PARTY CHAIRMAN

On learning that a general election had been called, Parnell abandoned the mission to return home reaching Queenstown on 21 March. For him, success at the hustings was paramount. While his North American visit had ensured that he was the foremost man in Ireland, his grip on the constituencies could by no means be taken for granted. In some places the clergy actively opposed Parnell's candidates, and he was able to oust only the most obdurate of sitting home rule MPs. The general election was held between 31 March and 13 April with Parnell's triple return for Cork City (5 April), County Meath (10 April) and County Mayo

(12 April); he chose to sit for Cork City, which remained his constituency for the rest of his life. Perhaps surprisingly in view of the agricultural depression and the dominance of the land question during the American tour, Parnell focused on the quality of parliamentary representation. At Dunboyne, County Meath, on 8 April he professed to believe that the tenant farmers would receive ameliorative legislation but 'the only way Ireland can obtain justice from any English government is by compulsion . . . You will get nothing from any Government, Whig or Tory, for love.'[18] He asserted that 'the only way in which you can succeed by Parliamentary methods of representation is to have an independent, determined, and active representation'.

Sixty-three (counting multiple returns) Home Rulers were elected and the Liberals took power; Gladstone would once more take the helm. At Cork city on 14 April Parnell commended the value of parliamentary representation and stated his expectation that Ireland would benefit most from the return of a substantial Liberal majority: 'I think Ireland has a far better chance with a large, really Liberal and Radical majority in the House of Commons than she would have if there was only a small Liberal majority.'[19] At this point Parnell had a strategy similar to Butt's in 1874, though with more bite. Butt had looked to an Irish contingent sufficiently numerous and united to influence a Liberal regime. His misfortune was to head a weak party, ill equipped to face a Conservative government unresponsive to Irish demands. The short period from between taking up the land issue and success at the general election was decisive in the making of a national leader who stood atop the political summit. Parnell completed the transformation begun in 1878 from a protest politician to an agenda-setter.

Up to this time Parnell had laid a claim to lead the Irish nation, but he did not have a leadership role in the parliamentary party. On

17 May 1880, however, he was elected party chairman over
William Shaw by 23 votes to 18. His intention was to concentrate
his own efforts at Westminster and leave the public agitation to
others. He spoke only once in Ireland between becoming party
chairman and 19 September. Events enforced a more aggressive role. The government failed to pilot the Compensation for
Disturbances Bill through the House of Lords, where it went
down to a crushing defeat on 3 August. This obliged Parnell to
assume the leadership of the agitation on the ground.

LAND AGITATION

Throughout the autumn of 1880 he lent his authority to an
increasingly radicalised struggle, but his own instincts and speeches
remained temperate. The agitation marked the third pivotal
incident in Parnell's career. He was astute enough to neither
confirm nor deny the motives which agrarian radicals attributed to
him. Yet he consistently held that the campaign must be legal,
dignified and non-violent. On 19 September at Ennis, he specifically
counselled that tenants who took a farm from which another had
been evicted should be shunned, treated as outcasts, but not
physically assaulted. In the same speech he emphasised the virtue of
parliamentarianism, independence from English ministries, and the
vitality of public opinion. He countered those who criticised parliamentary work, saying that the party in the session just concluded
was 'on the whole . . . a good and worthy one'.[20] Despite the
disappointment of the past session, he remained confident that
Parliament would legislate in the tenants' interest, cautioning:

> Depend upon it that the measure of the land bill of next session will be
> the measure of your activity and energy this winter – it will be the
> measure of your determination not to pay unjust rents – it will be the

measure of your determination to keep a firm grip of your homesteads. It will be the measure of your determination not to bid for
farms from which others have been evicted, and to use the strong force
of public opinion to deter any unjust men amongst yourselves – and
there are many such – from bidding for such farms. If you refuse to pay
unjust rents, if you refuse to take farms from which others have been
evicted, the land question must be settled, and settled in a way that will
be satisfactory to you. It depends, therefore, upon yourselves, and not
upon any commission or any government. When you have made this
question ripe for settlement, then, and not till then, will it be settled.

The land question was proving divisive within the national
coalition. At Galway on 24 October 1880 he sought to bridge the
growing rift, linking the land agitation to the national question:

> But large and important as is the class of tenant-farmers, constituting
> as they do with their wives and families, the majority of the people of
> this country, I would not have taken off my coat and gone to work, if I
> had not known that we were laying the foundations by this movement
> for the recovery of our legislative independence.[21]

Self-government, as he recognised, was the cement holding
national forces together. If the bonding weakened, the movement
would disintegrate.

Rapid escalation of the agrarian campaign in late 1880 and early
1881 presented Parnell with a dilemma. Public opinion in Britain
and moderates in Ireland held him accountable for atrocities he did
not condone and could not control. Despite receiving mass ador-
ation as a consequence of the struggle, he was relieved to escape
the public platform and return to the precincts of Westminster
Palace. Trouble awaited him there too.

The fierce conflict over the ministry's new special measures, the Protection of Person and Property Bill and the Arms Bill, in the early part of the parliamentary session of 1881, put Parnell in the spotlight as the Irish Party fought a rearguard action. The re-arrest of Michael Davitt on 3 February 1881 – he was free on parole – brought forth an emotional Parnellite response, culminating in the parliamentary suspension of several Irish MPs. Some wanted the party to voluntarily withdraw from Westminster and establish an alternative assembly in Dublin, a forerunner of Dáil Éireann in 1919, but both at the time of the original proposal and again in May, when the government began to arrest Land Leaguers under the Protection of Person and Property Act, Parnell declined to be drawn into this step.

His reluctance is sometimes seen as stemming from the necessity of remaining at Westminster to ensure the passage of the land bill. Parnell, in reality, was and remained a committed member of the House of Commons, and his refusal to desert it had deeper roots than the tactical advantage. When this bill was introduced on 7 April 1881, it threatened to splinter national ranks. Agrarian radicals thought it offered too little; they demanded that the bill be rejected. Moderates and tenant farmers largely accepted it. Several times Parnell attempted to close the gap. Initially he adopted the course of abstention on the second reading of the bill, though many of his party took exception to this strategy. At the Land League convention held in Dublin from 15 to 17 September 1881 he urged tenants to 'test' the act under the guidance of the Land League rather than rush into the newly established land courts. The formula broke down immediately, with priests, moderates and the tenant farmers ignoring this advice. Gladstone suspected Parnell's motives and inadvertently relieved the Irish leader from his predicament, having him arrested on 13 October and detained in Kilmainham jail. There Parnell remained until 2 May 1882, in comparative comfort as an untried suspect under the Protection of Person and Property Act. While in Kilmainham he was eager to discount rumours that 'we are involved in a treasonable conspiracy'.[22] He assured Katharine O'Shea, with whom he had begun an affair more than year earlier, of his distaste for the public agitation: 'At least, I am very glad that the days of platform speeches have gone by and are not likely to return. I cannot describe to you how hollow and wanting in solidarity everything connected with the movement was.'

Imprisonment doubly enhanced Parnell's status in Ireland, but he did not court martyrdom. He had no intention of being sacrificed to the 'cause'. In the spring of 1882 Parnell wanted to resolve the impasse with the government. If further legislation admitting many of those excluded from the land act were enacted, he believed the dispute could be resolved. That would allow Parnell 'to co-operate cordially for the future with the Liberal Party in forwarding Liberal principles and measures of general reform'.[23]

Throughout the land struggle Parnell had ample temptation to abandon parliamentarianism. The role of demagogue was superficially sweet. But however tempting he might find it, he was not swayed from pursuing Ireland's claims in Parliament. He saw the land campaign as the only available way to pressure the government to legislate. As his speeches reveal, he believed that public agitation alone would enable Irish Party MPs to gain passage of a land bill. As a small minority party, they had little parliamentary clout, and the option of directly winning votes in the House of Commons was scarcely viable. When the campaign had run its course, the main object achieved, Parnell not only shed his demagogue's cloak, but felt no impulse to resume platform politics until the divorce crisis.

CONCLUSION

Parnell's role in the House of Commons in 1880 and 1881 was not identical to that of the later 1870s. He continued to express national opinion and inform Parliament, while also teaching people at home and in Great Britain, but the Irish now entertained expectations of making an impress on legislation as well. Parnell spoke only occasionally on British and imperial issues during these years. In contrast to the situation in the 1870s, Irish questions were now at the centre of parliamentary affairs, and he devoted his energy to them.

CHAPTER 6

Parliamentary Politics
2 May 1882–22 October 1884

INTRODUCTION

Parnell had anticipated close co-operation with the Liberals in 1882 under the 'Kilmainham Treaty'. From this point onwards Parnell and Gladstone were the Siamese twins of the Irish Question, though not in quite the way anticipated by either man. H. C. G. Matthew observes, 'if Ireland was to be pacified, the leaders of constitutional opinion in Ireland would have to be accommodated and constitutionally within the general framework of the United Kingdom: it was therefore vital that the terms being set by those leaders should be terms which the United Kingdom as a whole could reasonably assent'.[1] The Prime Minister insisted that the decision to release the MPs and subsequently other uncharged suspects was a unilateral action by the government which no longer had grounds for their detention. But suspicions were inflamed by Captain O'Shea, husband of Katharine and MP for County Clare, who told W. E. Forster prior to his resignation as Chief Secretary 'that the conspiracy which has been used to get up boycotting and outrages will now be used to put them down', an idea that struck a chord in Gladstone, albeit from another angle.[2] The Kilmainham Treaty did not mark a change of course for Parnell. For him the Land War was a matter of necessity not an end in itself, whereas Davitt and others regarded the conflict as an opportunity to destroy landlordism and British rule. Yet the treaty set the mould for future arrangements. The immediate challenge was to contain the fissures in the nationalist coalition, a conundrum with or without the Phoenix Park murders. In the immediate context, the prospect of accord was damaged by the murders on 6 May 1882 of the new Chief Secretary, Lord Frederick Cavendish, and the Under-Secretary, Thomas Henry Burke.

COERCION AND ACCOMMODATION

In response to the murders, the government introduced a fresh coercion package, the Prevention of Crime Bill which was enacted on 12 July. Debates on the measure allowed Parnell to escape opprobrium for the Kilmainham Treaty. The return of Earl Spencer to the Lord Lieutenancy and the Crimes Act presented the Parnellites with the opportunity for a bifurcated approach to the Liberal government from May 1882. At Westminster, the Home Rulers could be a completely constitutional movement and establish links with other parties. Meanwhile in Ireland, by harrying the Irish administration they could prove their nationalist credentials and provide evidence for British opinion of the necessity of self-government. This suited Gladstone insofar as he and his government had no real, thought-out programme of reform for Ireland. A gap in perception could thus be encouraged to grow between the London and Dublin governments. Spencer, not Gladstone, could be seen to be the person in charge in Ireland. The odium of coercion, which *faute de mieux* was now the central feature of Liberal government in Ireland, could be made to fall on him. Spencer would become the pressure point in the case for home rule. Parnellites realised that the Chief Secretary, G. O. Trevelyan, who was not in the Cabinet, left the government of Ireland outside direct scrutiny in the House of Commons. This, indeed, had been one of Forster's aims in seeking to adjust his own position when a short time earlier he had advocated a reconstruction of the Irish Offices so that the Chief Secretary would operate beyond the reach of the House of Commons. Parnell on 28 June objected 'that there was no Chief Secretary for Ireland in the House with full powers to act'.[3] Spencer, he said, 'was saturated with the traditions of English government in Ireland, and the people of Ireland had no hope from his Administration'. Between 30 June and 1 July the party forced a 28-hour debate. This and other actions allowed Parnell and his troops to re-establish their combat credentials and to do so within the parliamentary forum. The other portion of the equation was amendment to the land legislation. The promised Arrears Act, allowing tenants in arrears and some leaseholders to apply to the land courts, passed on 18 August. Recent events had diverse outcomes. To Conservatives it began reflections about Ireland that had profound consequences. Five strands can be detected: an acceptance of land reform in the form of land purchase; social reconstruction; opposition to national self-government but willingness to implement democratic local government; refusal to engage directly with political nationalists but attempts to work with bishops and Catholic unionists; and to pinpoint nationalists and their British allies as covert supporters of agrarian violence. K. T. Hoppen points to the post-1867 consensus that Ireland required distinctly Irish remedies.[4]

Liberals, engaged in their own reappraisal, fell along an axis from resistance, accommodation, conciliation and co-operation.[5] The first does not imply uncompromising refusal to treat Irish wants, but relies heavily on the imposition and maintenance of security or coercion. Most governments under the Union relied upon some use of extra-ordinary legal instruments. The second – accommodation – was a policy of recognising distinctions and justifiable needs for Ireland, creating a sub-species of pluralism. A

third – conciliation – had prime objective of dividing Irish opinion
and enlisting a larger segment in support of the Union. And the
fourth – co-operation – sought to bring Irishmen and Englishmen
together for common objectives and, where necessary, to form a
front against British Conservative governments. Supporters of
the last often believed Anglo-Irish enmity would dissipate if Irish
people reached accord amongst themselves. While these categor-
ies were not mutually exclusive and opinion makers, including
Gladstone, shifted between them, they represent fundamentally
different approaches. Gladstone between 1882 and 1885 moved
towards co-operation, confusing many of his own supporters
and a considerable section of public opinion. Placed in this light,
Gladstone's Irish perambulation has fresh implications and bridges
some of the differences in the literature, in particular the analyses
finding his adoption of home rule inexplicable, sudden or conceived for extra-Irish reasons. His Irish perspective adapted Peelite
ideology into a distinctively Gladstonian formula. It was during
this period that a section of Liberalism accepted Parnellism as the
authentic voice of the Irish people, while a rearguard accepted the
need for reform but objected to dealings with nationalists.

   With passage of the new coercion and land acts the stage was set
for Parnell to unveil his strategy for the post-Kilmainham era: it
was remarkably reformist. At a personal level, he reverted to his
own commitment for advancing the interests of the evicted
tenants, agricultural labourers and urban working class, groups
who had gained little from the land war, and began advocacy of
Irish manufactures. For him the cornerstone of Ireland's economic
wants was employment and an equitable redistribution of income.
Better use of national resources would relieve under-employment
and emigration. At the banquet after receiving the Freedom of
Dublin on 16 August he stated: 'The only place in which we can
still venture, to a certain extent to speak our minds, with very strict

rules, is the House of Commons, and so long as that is left to us I propose to do my duty there.'[6] He predicted,

> I also think and feel confident that we are but at the commencement of the large measures of reform which may be expected for the masses of the people of Ireland. I think that the Land Act will in all probability be largely amended in the course of time. The Parliamentary and municipal suffrages will be extended in such a way as to give the people a fairer representation of their opinions, both in the Council Chamber and in the House of Commons.

He went on to say that Irish representation had been improved at the last general election but required further enhancement. So long as the prospect of reforms was present, 'I consent to remain a member of the British House of Commons for that end so long as it may be necessary for me to remain there, and no longer.' Then Parnell proceeded to laud the prospects of Irish manufactures, suggesting a form of voluntary protectionism by purchasing home-produced goods. The outcome, he claimed, would be to relieve endemic poverty of the labouring classes. A key though overlooked section of his address stressed 'that the Irish people have very moderate ideas as to the improvement of their condition'. He followed this with one of his last appeals of the old Butt-type for the Ascendancy to join with the people in national action:

> I would invite those who those who may be placed in the higher stations of life to trust to their Humber fellow-countrymen ... The advance of popular reform cannot be stopped for long even in Ireland, and it would be far better for the governing classes and for those in the higher ranks of society to trust the people of Ireland even at the eleventh hour, to join hands with them for the good of their common country. But if they will not do so, I am bound to say that we shall go on without them ...

On 21 August Parnell attended the Labour League and identified himself with its principal objective of securing housing and small plots of land for agricultural labourers. He blamed inaction not on farmers, as he would do later, but on the Board of Works for refusing loans for the construction of labourers' cottages. Advocating unity and organisation, he urged 'them to use it in such a moderate manner as will prevent any interference' by the authorities.[7]

In spite of, or perhaps as a consequence of the Phoenix Park murders, Gladstone received signals that Parnell wanted a fresh beginning. Katharine O'Shea visited him on 1 June and she subsequently called at Downing Street on 29 August and 14 September. Gladstone concluded 'that since his liberation he has acted ... with as much consistency as he could, and has endeavoured to influence his friends in the same direction'.[8] Moreover he rapidly became infatuated with the idea 'that the conspiracy which has been used to get up boycotting and outrages will now be used to put them down'. With time Gladstone became convinced that co-operation was the safest path which he translated into bolstering rather than attempting to undermine Parnell's influence. In Irish ranks, too, a division separated those who reverted to seeking material gains through co-operation with British parties and men who had got the taste for agitation and believed it was the best means to gain concessions. The latter wanted the land struggle to continue believing that thereby the British state would be brought to its knees. Parnell threw his authority behind the first section. The most important centre of opposition, Davitt, fortuitously began along a track that facilitated his marginalisation. On 6 June Davitt made his initial speech advocating land nationalisation, which was neither Land League dogma nor an idea that could appeal to the driving force of the land struggle, the farmers, town merchants and clergy.

Parnell also undermined the remnants of the Land League, gaining control over its funds deposited in Paris and also in August closed down the Ladies' Land League. The end and means by which he disbanded the Ladies' Land League caused permanent estrangement from his sister Anna.

From summer 1882 the Irish Party underwent reconstruction, evolving into a disciplined and effective institution. It also interacted with the localities in a more complete fashion. Weber describes the impetus: 'The driving force behind the progressive tightening of party ties was the interest which the members of parliament had in possible electoral compromise between localities, and in the effectiveness of unified electioneering in the country and of unified programmes accepted by broad sections of the country.'⁹ William Feingold suggests 'local politics generally remained outside of the sphere of jurisdiction of the national movement although . . . the activities of the local political groups were influenced by events on the national scene'.¹⁰ Virginia Crossman refines the point, noting a complex relationship between competing influences and observes that the success of the national movement was contingent upon maintaining not challenging existing class and gender inequalities.¹¹ Functioning through the National League, Parnellism adapted into a party of social integration, but within it there was tension between centralising and centrifugal forces, with a loose synthesis resulting in a strong centrally controlled parliamentary party and on the ground the dominance of the Catholic elite largely undisturbed by national imperatives. The synthesis facilitated a rural Catholic middle-class order wresting the local government of the country from the hands of the landlord classes. This aggression pre-dated the emergence of a disciplined party; it was parochial in origin and purpose but gained impetus and legitimacy from national events. Crossman notes that local government afforded tenants and rural businessmen opportunities for prestige, patronage, propaganda and capacity to reward friends or punish opponents.¹² Jim Mac Laughlin, employing Antonio Gramsci's 'organic

intelligentsia', treats nation building from below, showing that, as
the chief cultural/political entrepreneurs, the clergy with the aid
of schoolteachers invested the entire landscape with Catholic
nationalist symbolism.[13] Tom Garvin points out that within Irish
nationalism the 'green' or rural Catholic ethos struggled to gain
ascendancy over an urban, more cosmopolitan version of the
nation.[14] Davitt's private remark is propitious: 'if only Parnell knew
what local country leaders are *thinking* and *saying* he would pray to
be saved from his worshippers'.[15] Nationalists exploited old wounds
and the recent Land War as tools in the reshaping of Parnell's
ascendancy, but it was to be one containing rival components –
cosmopolitanism and the rustic – with 'The Chief' as the lynch-pin
holding it together. It is this which helps explain why his successors
were unable to reassemble the Parnell system after the Split.

At first Parnell was loath to sponsor any revival of a national
organisation. His experience of the chaotic Land League made
him chary; as a charismatic figure adept in manipulating public
sentiment he harboured suspicions of bureaucratic structures.
Ultimately, Parnell's personal indifference to organisations would
cost him dearly. However, the movement entered the phase which
Weber describes as the institutionalisation of the charismatic
leader's authority by his followers. The National Convention, held
on 17 October 1882, founded the Irish National League. Its programme – Home Rule, land reform and a considerable range of
social objectives – made this organisation the first national body to
promote a comprehensive agenda.[16]

The special autumn session of the House of Commons convened
(24 October to 2 December) to amend parliamentary procedure by
limiting the scope of small minorities to disrupt business. During
it, Parnell and his followers were able once again to use the stage of
Westminster to make Irish demands as well as pose objections to
proposed changes in parliamentary procedure. On 30 November

Parnell criticised restrictions on the privileges of members, denying obstruction of public business.[17] He pleaded, 'we in Ireland have at least as large an interest in facilitating the business of the House, so long as there is a prospect of obtaining for Ireland her fair share of remedial and beneficial legislation. That is the view which I have taken of the question of the business of the House.'

INSTITUTIONAL CONSOLIDATION

The following year, as Parnell had foreseen, lacked the excitement of the previous three parliamentary sessions, but it was a significant point of development for the party and for his own strategy. The orthodox interpretation is that Parnell sank to a nadir in 1883 and the party drifted to the right after 1882. Both necessitate qualification. The parliamentary session was more limited in intensity, if not by time, running from 15 February to 25 August. For a strategy focused on the House of Commons the implications of a more restricted diet of opportunities are obvious though, in fact, it marked a further extension of the Irish Party into British politics. Parnell was hampered by several constraints: the Prevention of Crime Act curtailed agitation in Ireland; the conviction and execution of the Invincibles for the Phoenix Park Murders cast a pall over Irish politicians; Gladstone's recuperation in Cannes from mid-January until early March left leadership to the Marquess of Hartington and a corresponding credibility void; and some fissures in support from marginal members of the party surfaced. Parnell, too, had the embarrassment of foreclosure on Avondale. A National Tribute to rescue his wounded finances was begun on 3 March and, in spite of being condemned by the Vatican in May, ended triumphantly in December. The prospect that Parnell, or at least certain of his close associates, were likely to be found connected to crime cannot be overestimated.

During 1883 Parnell threw his support behind legislation to facilitate construction of cottages for agricultural labourers. His support for labourers puts paid to five allegations. First, that he was intrinsically conservative; second that his support for labour in 1891 was a 'new-found' radicalism; third that he essentially ignored agricultural workers in favour farmers who possessed the ballot; fourth that he feared the impact of the labourers' vote in the extension of the franchise to this group in 1885; and fifth that the Irish Party under Parnell's guidance drifted to the right which would only be true if 'the right' were interpreted as meaning adherence to parliamentary forms which in any event had been its pre-land-war mode of operation.

The party itself was strengthened ideologically and organisationally by a handful of defections early in the year and it was to lose its last parliamentary election in the southern three provinces (outside Trinity College) during Parnell's time in March. In spite of a lack of a clearly defined programme before the session, 1883 was remarkably fruitful for Liberals and, as Parnell pointed out, for Ireland. Although Parnell made few public speeches in 1883 he addressed the House of Commons on innumerable topics, ranging from the land act, the labourers' question, franchise, Irish fisheries, and the Corrupt Practices Bill among other matters. His party took, if anything, an even more comprehensive approach to parliamentary business. Before 1883 the party normally acted on issues *ad hoc*, but at the beginning of the session it established 11 sub-committees to examine specific Irish bills. In May four more were established to examine the estimates, foreign and colonial affairs, local matters in Great Britain and the Irish Poor Law.

On 29 August 1883 Parnell explained his expectations to the National League convention. He defended his reluctance to formulate specific legislative schemes, holding fast to his 1870s belief in the expressive purposes of representation: 'I have always held that it was most undesirable for the Irish people to make proposals on such questions as Irish land and Irish self-government; but that we should, rather by agitation and organisation, set our English rulers and governors to work to consider these matters and to make their own propositions.'[18] 'I have every hope', he stated, 'that before long a measure in the direction of local self-government will be laid before Parliament; and though it may not go the whole distance that we go, yet undoubtedly, it will give considerable further powers to the Irish people.' He saw in responsible local government an opportunity to train the Irish people 'in those habits of self-government and self-reliance which are of so much advantage and of such vital importance in forming a nation'.

Parnell had been less than enthusiastic about reviving an Irish organisation in Britain, remembering its working-class and quasi-revolutionary propensities. At the end of September 1883 at a convention at Leeds it was reanimated, though under the strict control of the Irish Party and stewardship of T. P. O'Connor, who would be its long-serving President. Parnell did not speak again in public until receiving over £37,000 from the National Tribute on 11 December. On that occasion he attacked the administration of Spencer and Trevelyan, decreeing that co-operation with Liberals would be possible only when coercion and immigration ceased. However, his seeming militancy was punctuated by his praise of parliamentary action that would force the government to include Ireland in the anticipated extension of the franchise. He offered a spirited defence of representation: 'I am very much inclined to think that were it not for the fact that there exists in the House of Commons a solid band of 40 men who would vote steadily against any extension of the suffrage in England if Ireland were left out, we should see very little of the inclusion of Ireland in the bill.' Perhaps to assuage populist sentiment, he asserted, 'if we may not rule ourselves, we can at least cause them to be ruled as we chose'.[19]

In February 1884 the annual party meeting determined to present 12 bills including county government, extension of the municipal franchise, election of all Poor Law Guardians, voter registration, revision of the land laws and like measures. On 25 February Parnell objected to the limited time Ireland's needs were going to receive in the House of Commons. He submitted that 'so long as the English people and Parliament asserted their capability of legislating for the wants of Ireland that their first duty and care should be to carry out the obligation so undertaken'.[20]

On 6 April in London, Parnell underlined the growing stature of the Irish Party, claiming that many who had previously held aloof now looked to it as the fulcrum of national representation. He asserted that the party was the only 'efficient means for securing beneficial reform in Ireland'.[21] The tilt towards reformism seemed to be codified at Drogheda on 15 April where Parnell declaimed, 'the Irish land question, if it is to be settled by constitutional means, will have to be settled before the national question can be settled by constitutional means'.[22] In the same speech Parnell gave notice that his views on landlords had shifted since the 1870s. Whereas earlier he had wanted to solve the land question in a way that would enable his own order to assume its place in the nation, now Parnell increasingly saw the landlord class as an impediment to unity: 'The landlords of Ireland will have to be got rid of before we can hope to unite north and south, Catholic and Protestant, in such a way as to present our demands for national self-government constitutionally in an overwhelming fashion in the English Parliament.'

On 1 October the Catholic hierarchy passed a resolution asking the Irish Party to represent its education interest in the House of Commons. This seemed to fulfil Parnell's prognosis in early April that important groups increasingly looked to his party as the vehicle of beneficial reform. It also was an increment in the party being remoulded into a service institution, largely finalising transition into a party of social integration. Church, party and people were bonded into a mutually reinforcing socio-political culture. The Church was pivotal to the compound. Only it had the apparatus to maintain political mobilisation, freeing an elite party from the costly necessity of erecting a viable network of its own.

CONCLUSION

During 1882, 1883 and 1884 Parnell appeared in Ireland publicly only sporadically, though private stays at Avondale remained part of the annual calendar, and the party directed its energy towards specific reforms. In 1882 he appeared on public platforms seven times (five in Dublin, two in Cork), and during 1883 only on some dozen occasions, half of these occurring during the Monaghan by-election in June. During 1884 he spoke in public seven times (four in Ireland). Parnell extended his influence through the careful nurturing of journalists. Friendly reports in the press of party activities in the House of Commons sustained enthusiasm. Opportunities had changed, but Parnell continued to see Parliament as an instrument for expressive, teaching and informative functions; in addition, he increasingly sought ways to influence legislation, and in spite of a stated reluctance to draft bills the members of the party were doing so by 1884. This concentration on Westminster was novel for an Irish popular leader. O'Connell, though a parliamentarian, exerted his power through mass demonstrations. Parnell was a pioneer in the development of a different mode of political and social communication in Ireland – communication at a distance. Modernisation facilitated this novel style of leadership and communication. Catholics in Ireland now had high literacy and information was disseminated swiftly. For a man like Parnell, this innovative approach to moulding public opinion fitted his skills ideally. It could truly thrive only when genuine political competition was minimal and no great question divided the Catholic elite. In Ireland, in the years after mid-1882 these conditions were fulfilled.

CHAPTER 7

Home Rule
23 October 1884–8 June 1886

THE CONTEXT

By 1885 Parnell's strategy had succeeded; both the Liberal and Conservative parties had adopted land reform and were anticipating implementation of local self-government. In mid-1885 Parnell's position in the House of Commons took another leap forward. The Representation and Redistribution Acts of 1884–5 introduced uncertainty into British politics. Parnell's influence in Ireland's constituencies was assured; he seemed likely to gain the number of seats long considered an essential precondition for self-government to be taken seriously. Furthermore, his power in numerous British constituencies through the immigrant Irish vote was supposed to be substantial. By the mid-1880s the Irish Party had acclimatised itself to Westminster culture.

The high level of attendance and participation of the Irish Party in the House of Commons elevated its influence. Gladstone appreciated that Irish votes ordinarily supplemented Liberal numbers in divisions. There was common ground, particularly between Parnell's men and the progressive section of the Liberal Party. Conservatives, too, discovered that on questions such as education, land and religion an alliance with Parnell yielded benefits. In early June 1885 the Irish and Conservative parties jointly toppled Gladstone's second ministry.

By late 1885 Parnell had made inroads into Bagehot's one function that had thus far eluded him, the making and sustaining of ministries. Gladstone's conversion to Home Rule in 1886 appeared both at the time and subsequently to vindicate Parnell's tactics; it was the supreme triumph and fourth decisive chapter of his career. The success resulted from mustering Irish Catholics behind Parnell and his gaining a balance of power in the House of Commons.

But Parnell was confronted by a series of challenges. Some people in Ireland resented the dominance of a centralised party apparatus and tried during 1885 to assert local authority over the selection of parliamentary candidates. A few colleagues were restive at Parnell's leadership, believing themselves better suited to head the movement. Agrarian radicals were hostile to land purchase legislation even though it was an aim of Parnell and of the Land League. Alternative interests such as the nearly forgotten House League intruded on the public scene, seeking redress of their own grievances. The House League, formed in 1885, included among its objectives the reduction of rackrents in urban residential accommodation.[1] However, unlike tenanted land, Catholics were more frequently the landlords of this urban property and thus the movement portended a division in the national ranks. This and other fractures enforced upon Parnell his formula of emphasising the overarching primacy of the one common bond, national self-government. Five aspects of the home rule crisis merit close attention – chronology and context; the contextual and semantic meaning of self-government; the intersection of ideas, ideology and Christian motivation with imperatives of institutional structures; the discourse about governmental forms, majoritarian rights and notions of citizenship; and the imaginative responses of politicians. The period has importance in several areas:

- It showed that even at the height of his popularity Parnell's authority was not uncontested;
- Although at the pinnacle Parnell exerted considerable influence in British politics, real power lay in the hands of the key figures of the two leading parliamentary parties;
- Constitution making was a complex process;
- The obstacles to home rule were enormous.

FRANCHISE EXTENSION AND LOCAL GOVERNMENT

The dramatic events between the fall of Gladstone's ministry in June 1885 and the defeat of the Home Rule Bill in June 1886 could not have been anticipated as 1884 drew to a close. Parnell had good reason to be optimistic about the future, but his concrete expectations were still modest. In December 1884 he wrote to Archbishop Croke of Cashel of the importance he assigned to the extension of the franchise and his 'hope that we may be able to follow this up next session by laying the foundations of a wide and comprehensive scheme of local government'.[2] Parnell knew from Gladstone's public statements and contacts with Joseph Chamberlain that local self-government was assuming a prominent place in Liberal Party thinking. He was anxious that it be understood that 'we do not propose this local self-government plank as a substitute for the restitution of our Irish Parliament but solely as an improvement of the present system of local government in Ireland. The claim for restitution of Parliament would still remain.'[3]

During January 1885 tensions within the national movement surfaced. A brief rebellion against the party nominee for the County Tipperary parliamentary by-election was augmented by criticism of Parnell's alleged lack of fidelity to Home Rule. On 8 January 1885 he indicated how the 'true' representation of Irish interests would be advanced by the current franchise reforms: 'For the first time it will be in your power to have your thoughts, wishes, and aspirations truly respected in an alien Parliament. For the first time your representatives will act and think as you act and think – for the first time they will reflect the true opinion of the masses of the Irish people.'⁴ At Clonmel, County Tipperary, on 9 January, and then more famously at Cork city on the 21st, Parnell attempted to allay criticism of the movement, stressing the inviolate character of national self-government. On the second occasion he uttered the often-quoted phrase 'No man has the right to fix the boundary to the march of a nation; no man has a right to say to his country: "Thus far shalt thou go and no further", and we have never attempted to fix the *ne plus ultra* to the progress of Ireland's nationhood, and we never shall.'⁵ By reasserting the primacy of Home Rule, Parnell returned again, as he would later in the year, to his practised formula when faced by dissension.

Local government reform proved as contentious as the land question. It stumbled on into May 1885, when it was rejected by the cabinet. On 20 May Lord Randolph Churchill signalled that his party would be prepared to dispense with the Prevention of Crime Act. In the early hours of 9 June the government was defeated and later in the month replaced by a minority Conservative regime. The circumstances were exceptional. Because of the need to compile a fresh electoral register, a general election could not be held for several months. It seemed as though the Parnellite parliamentary strategy had reached fruition and the Irish Party had secured a central place in the political process. Nationalists crowed about their new-found influence. Parnell discovered that in many areas he could work with a Tory ministry. A common thread between Earl Spencer and Lord Carnarvon, the new Viceroy, was that both men were driven by administrative imperatives emanating from officials in Dublin Castle. It was a covert and largely unrecognised avenue for the arrangement of public affairs and one into which Parnell, leading nationalists, ecclesiastics and other influential figures were now incorporated by both of the British party elites. Spencer had enlisted Catholics and nationalists into the Irish administration: the solicitor, George Fottrell, one such appointment, opened a conduit to key nationalists and was perhaps 'the earliest example of the Liberal policy of "greening" Dublin Castle in anticipation of Irish home rule'.[6] Overall, the circumstances created an intoxicating cocktail that went to the head of some participants. At a secret meeting on 1 August with the Viceroy, Carnarvon, Parnell learned that a Conservative cabinet would concede about as much as the Liberals; Carnarvon heard at first hand that the Irish leader's demands were sufficiently limited that a Tory government could accommodate him. Lord Salisbury's ministry passed three major Irish bills, the most important being land purchase legislation which provided £5 million for tenants to buy their holdings. Meanwhile Gladstone did not sit by idly. On 14 July his son Herbert made a speech in favour of Home Rule and, through the Chief Whip's exchanges with Mrs O'Shea, the Liberal leader sought to learn what institutional reforms Parnell would accept. For the time being nothing came of this overture, but Parnell knew in the summer of 1885 that both British parties were ready to make concessions.

However, he did not have a clear field. On 15 August Michael Davitt denounced the recently passed land purchase legislation.[7] Adding to his own difficulties Parnell raised many eyebrows when at Arklow on the 20th he advocated protection for some Irish manufactures.[8] Then William O'Brien, Home Rule MP for Mallow and editor of the nationalist newspaper *United Ireland*, poured oil on the flames when he suggested that National League branches should set the 'fair price' to be paid by tenants and boycott anyone who offered more.[9] On 25 August Parnell responded to these interjections at a banquet in Dublin, stating that the party stood before the country on 'a platform with one plank only, and that one the plank of national independence'.[10] Resolution of other questions, he said, must await the establishment of self-government.

Two other problems complicated the situation. Healy spearheaded a backstairs intrigue against Parnell's leadership, portraying him to the English Radical MP Henry Labouchere as merely a phantom leader. William Walsh, the new Archbishop of Dublin began his own machinations to bypass Parnell.

In October 1885 Parnell directed that a draft document on Home Rule be prepared, and he provided a copy for Gladstone, hoping for some positive response from the Liberal leader. Gladstone was unwilling to make a commitment before the general election.

Altogether he attended and spoke at seven nominating conventions. Parnell's largest number of speeches were in Liverpool where he attempted unsuccessfully to secure Captain O'Shea a seat and in Louth where he ousted Philip Callan (five in each versus eight during the rest of the campaign). During this second election Callan raised publicly Parnell's relationship with Mrs O'Shea. At Wicklow on 5 October Parnell declared once more that the platform had 'a single plank, that plank being legislative independence'.[11] He repeated his insistence that it must be 'a parliament that shall have power to protect Irish manufactures if it be the will of that parliament and of the Irish people that they should be protected'. In an interview with the *New York Herald* on 10 October he repeated the necessity of protection and, interestingly, that he expected the Liberals to go further than the Conservatives in satisfying Irish wants.[12] At the Kildare convention on 11 October he urged landlords to avail themselves of the opportunity to sell the land to tenants, the Ashbourne Act being a 'golden bridge to escape from an untenable position'.[13]

On 21 November the Irish National League of Great Britain issued a manifesto calling upon its countrymen to vote against the Liberals and Radicals. Only a handful of candidates were exempted from this controversial proclamation. When balloting ended on 9 December, the Liberals had won 335 seats, the Conservatives 249, the Irish Party 86, including 85 of Ireland's 103 constituencies (in Ulster 17, a majority of one). T. P. O'Connor's election in Liverpool accounts for the one victory outside the country. Parnell's force exactly equalled the difference between the British parties. His impact on the outcome in Great Britain was less clear. Possibly, the much vaunted Irish vote determined the outcome of a handful of constituencies. Parnell to be sure possessed greater influence, but he could only obtain Irish objectives with the aid of one of the British parties; he needed Gladstone more than Gladstone needed him.

On 17 December Gladstone's son, Herbert, announced that his father had been converted to home rule. During December 1885 and January 1886 Parnell tried to elicit some commitment from Gladstone on self-government. The Liberal chief deflected these advances, eventually taking office at the beginning of February 1886 on the very restricted pledge 'to examine whether it is or is not practicable to comply with the desire... for the establishment... of a legislative body, to sit in Dublin, and to deal with Irish as distinguished from imperial affairs'.[14]

At this juncture Parnell faced another challenge. Captain O'Shea's efforts to secure an English constituency at the general election had failed. Parnell now insisted that he be selected as the unpledged Irish Party candidate for the vacancy at Galway borough. By this time Parnell's relationship with Katharine O'Shea was well-known in political circles. A handful of MPs, including Healy, were determined to thwart the candidacy. The rebellion was eventually confounded, but only when Parnell declared that it would endanger Home Rule. Now he desperately needed a substantial proposal from Gladstone.

HOME RULE

On 8 April 1886 Gladstone introduced a parliamentary bill embodying a scheme by which Ireland would be given virtual autonomy over domestic affairs. Parnell was not consulted over its drafting, and he expressed reservations about certain provisions. Nevertheless, it was a substantial measure. It was devised to enforce co-operation between the two Irelands – or at least between a predominantly Catholic rural bourgeoisie and a southern Protestant propertied class. It held few attractions for Ulster Protestants. Gladstone's proposal granted virtual autonomy over domestic affairs. While he declared that it was not a finished scheme, only minor details were left open.[15] Exclusions fell under three main headings: the powers of the Crown; defence; and foreign and colonial affairs. The Irish Parliament had the power to raise revenue though not to impose custom duties. From a constitutional perspective, the plan had three defects – it failed to deal with Irish representation at Westminster after home rule; revenue-raising authority was not dealt with adequately; and no satisfactory rationale for the continued supremacy of the British Parliament was provided.[16] Parnell expressed reservations about imperial retention of customs duties; Ireland's financial contribution; failure to handover immediately control of the Royal Irish Constabulary; and separate voting of the two orders of the Irish Parliament. Nevertheless, it was a substantial proposal, reflecting the underlying ideology of both Gladstone and Parnell. In the latter's words, 'whatever may be the fate of the measure, the cause of Irish autonomy will have gained enormously in a way it never could otherwise have gained by the genius of the right hon. Gentleman'.[17]

In order for the project to succeed eight identifiable groups or portions of these had to be persuaded. (1) The national movement had to convince the Catholics of Ireland; (2) implementation required adoption by a major British party; (3) the House of Commons had to pass the measure; (4) opposition in the House of Lords would have to be overcome; (5) British public opinion required assurances; (6) significant press support was essential; (7) southern Irish Unionists' resistance and concomitant influence in the Upper Chamber had to be moderated; and (8) Ulster Unionist interests had to be satisfied. The ensuing set of events only managed to meet the first two requirements.

The arguments for and against national self-government were voluminous but a brief summary delineates the terrain. Advocates maintained (1) that the Irish were a historic people seeking self-determination with the general election confirming their sentiments; (2) granting home rule would solidify not weaken Ireland's connection with Great Britain and this would no longer be based on force rather than consent; (3) respect of social order was undermined at present because laws were not made by those who commanded public respect; (4) Westminster-made laws had failed; (5) coercion was a discredited policy and current disorder necessitated a new programme acceptable to the Irish; (6) local government reform alone was not satisfactory to Irish opinion; (7) some questions, notably education and land, required an intermediate body to protect the British Exchequer; (8) removal of Irish business from Westminster could facilitate the operation of British democracy and enable Parliament to exercise its proper functions; (9) the bill contained adequate safeguards for the minority and ensured the supremacy of Parliament; (10) home rule promised 'finality'; a mere slate of concessions would not be a cure and could exacerbate the present cancer and (11) Irish self-government was an increment in fashioning world order and peace. Binding all this together was the

Liberal recognition of the dignity and virtue of the common people; support for home rule was a means of expressing these qualities.

Pitted against home rule was an equally impressive case. Its chief elements were that (1) the Liberal–Parnellite version of history was flawed; (2) Ireland may have been misgoverned earlier but this had been corrected and further improvements were in the pipeline; (3) the Irish were not a 'distinct' nationality and indeed there was in reality two Irelands; (4) it was incorrect to posit a stark choice between coercion and home rule; (5) foreign analogies could not be applied; (6) a Dublin Parliament would seek separation; (7) the National League was a menace to property; (8) the loyal minority would be in danger; (9) Gladstone's bill was structurally unsound; and (10) home rule meant Rome rule. Opponents insisted that a constitutional measure of this significance required an electoral mandate and it had not been placed before the voters in 1885. Many declared in favour of reform in Ireland and support for local self-government. The alleged suddenness of the scheme was a telling argument; a weakness was the reluctance to recognise Irish national identity.

Gladstone declined to consider special provision for the north-east, while on 7 June Parnell rejected it, stating: 'We cannot give up a single Irishman.'[18] Less notice is given to his other reasons. He declared that inclusion of northern Protestants was vital for the security of the southern minority and that a substantial Protestant contingent in an Irish parliament would be a bulwark against the ambitions of the Catholic Church to control education. In the early hours of 8 June the Home Rule Bill was defeated on its second reading by 341 votes to 311.

IMPACT OF THE CRISIS

The Home Rule Bill elevated Parnell's stature, but it also altered his influence. Three outcomes merit emphasis for they played a key part in Parnell's weakness in the later split. First, Parnell's freedom to choose between parties was curtailed. It reinforced his disposition towards parliamentarianism, enabling him to whip critics into line. Home Rule would only come from Liberal hands; Parnell had therefore to pursue a course consistent with Liberal susceptibilities. But Gladstone's age (he was born in 1809), and the reality that there might not be another general election for seven years, added to his problems. In 1890–1 Parnell clearly lost the argument that the party had to be completely independent. The reality was, as Crossman points out, that although the alliances were not inevitable, Conservatives were locked into an alliance with Irish landlords and Liberal Unionists, just as nationalism was imprisoned by Liberals.[19] Second, as James H. Murphy observes, the crisis induced 'an ideological realignment in the language of adherence to the Crown . . . a strengthening of the cohesion of notions of loyalty to the Crown and support for the Union'.[20] This bore on the perception in the split that Parnell meant to tread an alternative path from the post-1886 consensus and this threatened the still insecure respectability of middle-class Catholics. And, third, Reinhard Bendix suggests that political agitation aims at the political integration of an excluded people; it may shift from demanding integration to changing the community in order to make full citizenship possible.[21] The Home Rule episode significantly shifted the Irish sense of being an excluded people. Parnell's challenge appeared to undermine his own insistence that he had brought the mass of Irish people within the Constitution.

CHAPTER 8

The Plan of Campaign and the Conservatives
9 June 1886–17 November 1890

THE SCENE

The years between the defeat of the Home Rule Bill and the divorce crisis have received less attention than earlier parts of Parnell's career or the months following the divorce court verdict. Differing constructions have been placed on Parnell's actions, ranging from his error of judgement in not supporting the renewed rural agitation, the exigencies of the Liberal alliance, emphasis on the subtlety of his strategy, and/or that the strategy was flawed in the face of Conservative initiatives. The key elements of these years can be summarised:

- Limited options open to a constitutional movement;
- Parnell's increasingly chronic health problems;
- Growing assertiveness of the localist Catholic culture;
- Problems of maintaining the Liberal alliance
- Skilful and adaptive approach of the Conservative-Liberal Unionist coalition;
- Threat to link Parnell or at least some prominent supporters to outrage and crime during the earlier Land War.

In Ireland, Parnell's stature remained pre-eminent through the continued adept exploitation of the press which, since the obstruction episode of the 1870s, brought his mystique to virtually every Irish hearth. His stature was embellished by an impressive expansion of a provincial press that was increasingly nationalist and Catholic after 1886. Newspapers claiming links to the Catholic Church were expanding in number while gains in literacy were greatest in the poorer west where the appetite for nationalist newspapers and their circulation rose correspondingly. Journalists likewise rose numerically with Catholics benefiting from swelling demand. Parnell, who was never a demagogue, saw himself as the leader of a parliamentary party, a role which fitted him and he played with continued effect, in part due to the continuing communications revolution.

GENERAL ELECTION

In the face of defeat in the House of Commons, Gladstone on 10 June called a general election. Tories opposed Gladstone's proposal but most key figures, as in the instance of the party leader, Salisbury, on 18 June, advocated reform in Ireland, notably the extension of local government.[1] Sir Michael Hicks Beach affirmed that 'it should be our guiding principle to equalise as far as possible political privileges or disabilities throughout the United Kingdom'.[2]

During the campaign Parnell spoke eight times, all in England and Wales. He attempted to reassure audiences that home rule did not mean separation and that nationalists accepted the bill as a final solution. He again rejected a separate parliament for north-east Ulster. On 26 June at Plymouth he reverted to the land question: 'If you give the right of self-government to Ireland the Irish land question will be settled by the Irish legislature upon terms which the Irish landlords have not deserved by their past conduct.'[3] At Chester on the 29th Parnell maintained that the Home Rule Bill 'is not everything that we asked for, but we recognise in it a fair offer, and which taken in connexion with the friendly feeling between the two democracies, would lead to a final settlement of this question'.[4] His pledge of a 'final settlement' proved controversial. On the 31st at Wrexham in an attempt to defuse concerns that home rule spelt a rupture of the constitution, Parnell contended, 'a constitution for Ireland, therefore, would mean nothing more but such a modification or alteration of the British Constitution as would allow Ireland to have Parliamentary representative institutions of her own.[5] Finally, on 3 July at a rally at London Fields, he summed up the national and land questions, expressing his faith in Gladstone's commitment to do justice to Ireland.[6]

Balloting took place between 1 and 17 July, but it was quickly apparent that 'justice to Ireland is not very enticing to the English'.[7] A swing of 5.7 per cent against the government in the popular vote under the new electoral system exaggerated the parliamentary arithmetic; the Liberals won 191 seats, the Irish Party retained 85, while Conservatives and Liberal Unionists returned to the new Parliament with a total of 394. Unionists had 118 unopposed returns. As in the previous summer, there was a generous amount of uncertainty. Salisbury indicated this when saying they 'were returned with one mandate – to maintain the union'.[8] Gladstone's age raised doubts whether he would see another general election which might not take place for seven years. Ironically, Parnell not Gladstone entered his last Parliament. Salisbury's new Cabinet was not intent upon reaction but rather characterised by its caution; Hicks Beach's return to Ireland as Chief Secretary was on the understanding that he might be able to do good.[9]

After 1886 Parnell emphasised the efficacy of the constitution and propounded a Whiggish interpretation of Ireland's linear progression away from quasi-revolution – a progression that he would assert was endangered by the Conservative government's abrogation of fundamental rights in Ireland. Integral to Parnell's view was the value he attached to the extension of the franchise, allowing Ireland's voice to be properly heard at Westminster. His position was altered by the home rule episode, though initially it was unclear in precisely what ways other than no longer having the theoretical option to choose between British parties.

From September 1886 to December 1890 Parnell addressed public audiences on only seven occasions and none of these were in Ireland. His forum was the House of Commons, where, except during spells of illness, he continued to participate in major debates. He continued to visit his estate, particularly in the grouse-shooting season, albeit less frequently than earlier.

SIR MICHAEL HICKS BEACH

Parnell was confronted with five difficulties in the early months of the new government – growing crime and agrarian disturbances; potential Liberal rebellion over any forthcoming Tory land scheme which potentially Parnell might support; agrarian radicals who were immune to restraint; less than subtle challenges from ecclesiastics and others within his own movement; and pressure from Liberal leaders to allow modification of the home rule proposal.

Parnell received an ominous warning of trouble ahead when an interview with Archbishop Walsh appeared in the Dublin press between 10 and 16 August. The prelate made a thinly veiled attack on the secular leadership and, in effect, announced his own agenda. Emmet Larkin posits the thesis of a clerical–nationalist alliance where the Irish Party accepted the leadership of the hierarchy on education while the bishops recognised Parnell and the party as the political organ of the nation in secular affairs. His hypothesis exaggerates the degree of clerical subordination and political collusion of Church and party. Walsh signalled the division, affirming that 'sweeping reductions in rent' as an 'absolute necessity just now', supported the idea of land nationalisation, and offered his own thoughts on a future home rule solution while at the same time levelling an unfavourable riposte to Parnell's 'final settlement': 'For my own part,' he stated, 'I must say that I was a little surprised at the readiness with which that pledge was given, as regards the acceptance of certain portions of Mr Gladstone's bill. Personally I could not have been a party to the giving of it.'[10]

Parnell's predicament was not relieved when Parliament convened on 19 August and the approach of the Salisbury government proved to be muted. The Queen's Speech hinted at improving enforcement of the law but concentrated on the questions of local government, land legislation and improvement of Ireland's economy.[11] A commission chaired by Lord Cowper was established to investigate the land problem and the development of Irish industry. Hicks Beach stated that his aim was 'a policy which has for its great object the social and the material welfare of Ireland'.[12] Parnell's response criticised the expenditure of public money for the development of industrial resources, 'the best and only way to develop the industrial resources of Ireland is to allow the Irish people to do all these works themselves'.[13] However, his main focus was on the immediate rural condition and he closed with an amendment to the address: 'We fear that, owing to the heavy fall in prices of agricultural products, the greatest difficulty will be experienced during the coming winter by the Irish tenant farmers in the payment of their present rents and many will be unable to pay these rents.' He called for the suspension of evictions. When the Cowper Commission reported in February it proved a major increment to resolution of the land question and provided precisely the legitimisation necessary to proceed with legislation. Following debate on 26 and 27 August Parnell's amendment was heavily defeated. Afterwards he warned, 'neither the Irish members nor the government had any control over events which might occur in

Ireland during the months of winter'.[14] Yet he 'desired that it should not be supposed that . . . he was going to again to lead such an agitation as took place in the winter of 1880'. At the dinner for Justin McCarthy on 8 September Parnell reminded the nation that there is 'considerable responsibility upon us not to lose or forfeit any of the vantage ground that we have gained. We can be more moderate than we were in '79 or '80 because our position is very much stronger.'[15] The Irish people, he believed, 'will recognise this, that they will use those weapons of legality and moderation which have distinguished their cause up to the present'. In an interview published on 11 September Parnell spoke of the inevitability of home rule but mainly focused on the land problem and appealed to America to assist the evicted tenants. Parnell insisted that he did not desire large-scale state finance for Irish projects, only the freedom to develop Ireland's resources: 'I don't believe in developing Irish industries by state aid.'[16] On 20 September he introduced his Tenants' Relief Bill which would suspend evictions where a tenant paid one-half of his rent due in 1886 and one-half of any earlier arrears or, in the cases where genuine insolvency was proved, admit leaseholders to the Land Act of 1881, and give the Land Courts power to reduce judicial rents fixed before 31 December 1884. Although Gladstone spoke in favour of the bill on the second reading, he and many Liberals did not like the measure and were undoubtedly relieved by its demise. Conservatives were not of a mind to make concessions to Parnell and the Tenants' Relief Bill met its expected fate on 24 September.

Parnell had survived the first test of holding the alliance with the Liberals and keeping agitation within the law. In spite of his minority position Parnell was blessed with a situation where he was able to appear effective and in charge of the agenda, an appearance that persisted throughout the months of Hicks Beach's reign. The Chief Secretary had sympathy for the tenants, was limited by the legal tools at his disposal, the government lacked a defined Irish policy, and Salisbury's Cabinet was divided on Ireland and other matters. Parnell did not have a clear run; indeed, he was swiftly put under fresh pressure by agrarian radicals. The Plan of Campaign, published on 23 October in *United Ireland*, advocated that tenants on estates combine to offer the landlord a portion of the rental and, if refused, to lodge it with trustees of good repute. Tenant compliance required the use of the boycott: 'farms unjustly evicted will be left severely alone, and everyone who aids the victims shunned'.[17] Laurence Geary observes that though the Plan was a response to specific circumstances, it 'had an implicit political role . . . its purpose was no less than the extirpation of land-lordism.'[18] He emphasises that 'it was not alone an attack on the institution of landlordism but, in the wake of the rejection of the Home Rule Bill, it was for many an attack on the landlord class as part of the English garrison in Ireland, underlining once again the close relationship between land and nationalism'.

It is scarcely surprising, then, that the government interpreted it as an insurrection. During the autumn Parnell was ill and health problems would plague him during his remaining life. He was not comfortable with the Plan of Campaign, repeatedly said that he had not been consulted about its implementation but criticised the government for failing to tackle the agrarian problem thereby making it necessary. Implicit in Parnell's attitude was his realisation that behind the Plan and its attack upon the legitimacy of rent and landlordism was a threat to home rule. Plan organisers were drawn from the more radical elements of the nationalist movement while the local leadership was supplied by the parochial clergy, who often originated from the tenant farmer strata, fuelling the anti-landlord and anti-Protestant prejudices of their flock. The Plan was an almost exclusively Catholic movement, confirming a congruence of socio-economic and religious-national fault lines. As Parnell anticipated, the Plan itself proved divisive both within the national movement and between it and the Liberals. As yet the government and Irish administration continued to respond cautiously, while Hicks Beach attempted to get landlords to eschew evictions, grant rent abatements and delayed government assistance to those who declined to comply. The Irish Administration reacted to the growing menace by prosecutions of William O'Brien and John Dillon but failed to slow the progress of the agitation. By the end of November the Plan of Campaign was in operation on a dozen estates.

From early November into February the Chief Secretary and Archbishop Walsh were in friendly communication about education and had two private interviews in December and a further one in the first week of January. On 2 December Walsh endorsed the Plan. Initially, the Plan enjoyed the element of surprise and novelty. Yet a persistent problem was the linguistic flamboyance of the chief organisers. Dillon, not one to guard his tongue, on 5 December set off alarm bells. In its aftermath Parnell and John Morley met twice (the first with Spencer in tow) about Liberals' reaction to the agitation and he found that 'in England the effect is wholly bad'.[19] A second matter was raised as a consequence of projected discussions between Gladstonians, Joseph Chamberlain and G. O. Trevelyan, to effect a Liberal reunion, a unity that presupposed concessions to Chamberlain's position on devolved government.[20] It was a huge challenge to Parnell, propelling urgency in drawing a line round the operations of the Plan of Campaign. According to O'Brien, Parnell insisted that the leaders 'should set bounds to your operations' to which the first reassured him of their intention to confine the Plan to selected estates.[21]

The Queen's Speech on 28 January drew attention to the deteriorating condition of Ireland and the intention to seek additional legal powers. Parnell's reply on 7 February urged the

government to admit leaseholders to the provisions of the Land
Act of 1881. In his answer to the address he acknowledged the
constructive role of the Plan of Campaign.[22] He maintained that
'where the Plan had been adopted by all the tenantry, is very good
testimony to the circumstances that instead of leading to outrages
it has pacified the country'. Parnell's well-balanced statement gave
no hint of his future role in the Plan though the government would
not be giving his comments an unwarranted reading, if they supposed that he might take a much wider part or at least offer more
forceful encouragement. On 17 February he returned to the cause
of the leaseholders and also challenged the proposed amendment
to the rules of the House of Commons aimed at curtailing the
powers of minorities.[23]

The Cowper Commission reported on 21 February, recom-
mending the admission of leaseholders to the Land Act of 1881,
reduction in the length of judicially fixed rents and, where
suitable, adjustment of existing rentals. For Salisbury the revision
of rents was 'the price we have to pay for the Union and it is a very
heavy one'.[24] The recommendations met the main points Parnell
raised the previous year, entrenching his reluctance to lead the
Plan of Campaign.

The first months of Unionist rule had brought Parnell considerable satisfaction. He had succeeded in holding together his own
coalition. Liberals had stayed firm and the Conservatives, as yet,
had not formulated a convincing Irish approach to undermine
nationalism or to reassure Irish Unionists. Parnell was able to
appear proactive. At the beginning of March 1887 he appeared as
pivotal as he had been a year earlier.

BALFOUR'S ADMINISTRATION UNTIL THE SPECIAL COMMISSION

Arthur Balfour became Chief Secretary on 7 March, bringing a fresh touch to the Irish Office. Instilling Unionism with a burst of self-confidence and formulating schemes designed for social and economic advancement, Balfour's reign marked a shift away from conciliation and towards a mixture of security, co-operation with anti-nationalists and accommodation of Catholic interests. Most of all Balfour was an agenda-setter who negated Parnell's ability to hold the initiative. L. P. Curtis, jnr, catalogues a parcel of measures designed to improve procedures of the Irish administration; encourage landowners; prosecute agitators; subject political prisoners to ordinary prison rules; arrest participating priests; enforce the law against the press; employ the courts to impose strains on Plan of Campaign funds; effect contacts with the papacy; and initiate the Special Commission on Parnellism and Crime to discredit the nationalist movement and show its connection with criminality.[25] Crossman observes that the distinction between Hicks Beach and Balfour was 'more a matter of style than substance'; Balfour's achievement lay in allowing anti-home rulers to justify their refusal to countenance Irish Party demands because they emanated from a small group of self-serving and power-hungry individuals prepared to use any means to attain their ends.[26] His hallmark was 'repression as stern as Cromwell, reform as thorough as Mr Parnell or anyone else can desire'.[27] Balfour thought that land purchase was the ultimate solution to the land question but recognised as well that the country's economic deficiencies, particularly in the west, had to be redressed. His approach was not applied systematically and indeed was piecemeal in ideology and implementation, but also represented an optimistic belief that Catholics could be won over to the Union though this was seen as a long-run possibility.

Curtis points to coercion, nullifying the effects of conciliation; Andrew Gailey casts doubt on whether there was anything resembling a coherent conciliation approach; Margaret O'Callaghan finds a consistent and effective policy lodged in Balfour's refusal to distinguish between different kinds of 'patriot' – by equating Parnellism with crime, he stymied the Home Rule movement.[28] She contends that Parnell's brand of constitutionalism was dead even before the divorce scandal. Balfour's approach must be seen as evolutionary rather than a cogent plan from the outset. It had two phases separated by the Special Commission.

Parnell's stance now required recalibration. Although principally the head of a parliamentary party, he was also the leader of the 'nation', carrying a differing set of expectations. Until mid-1888 Parnell's approach to the Plan of Campaign was open-ended. By then he adjudged correctly that the 'nation' was anything but unified on the Plan, while the excesses of Dillon and O'Brien and the increasing assertiveness of Balfour rendered his participation contrary to the interests of the party and country. On 7 March, the day that Balfour became Chief Secretary, *The Times* published the first of a series of articles titled 'Parnellism and Crime'. These pieces changed the dynamics of the political world.

During March 1887 Parnell fought tenaciously against changes in House of Commons procedure. Meanwhile, *The Times* continued its series of allegations. Balfour on 28 March introduced the Criminal Law and Procedure Bill, giving the Irish Executive permanent emergency authority, subject to parliamentary review, over designated or proclaimed disaffected districts, and the power to deal summarily with conspiracies for withholding rents, acts of boycotting, intimidation, resistance to evictions and similar activities. Nationalists, including Parnell, acted with great vigour in opposition to the bill. Owing to illness from the beginning of April Parnell was largely absent from the House of Commons until early June. On 18 April *The Times* published what purported to be a facsimile letter of Parnell's sympathising with the murder of T. H. Burke in 1882: 'I cannot refuse to admit that Burke got no more than he deserved.'[29] In the same issue the newspaper challenged Parnell to issue 'more solid proofs, if he is to annul the effect of a disclosure which reduces the passionate denials with which his party encounter unpleasant truths.' In the House of Commons Parnell immediately denounced the authenticity of the letter, but he was undeniably under a cloud.[30]

On his return to politics in June Parnell remained an active in the House of Commons until the close of the session in September. By mid-year Parnell faced several threats concurrently. His own agrarian activists were reckless, Liberals mistrusted the projected land legislation, the movement was rocked back on its heels due to the allegations by *The Times*, the Vatican dispatched its own emissaries to assess the situation in Ireland, and the fall in the value of agricultural output was not arrested. In the wake of a stream of disturbing reports and intrigues, the Vatican dispatched Monsignor Persico and Fr Gualdi to Ireland; they arrived on 8 July. In his only public speech during the year directed at his own activists as much as Gladstonians, Parnell at the National Liberal Club on 20 July, the day after the Criminal Law and Procedure Act [Jubilee Act] had been passed, attempted to defuse as much of the difficulty as possible, carefully balancing praise for Gladstone and the Liberal Party with criticism of the Conservative government. It was a delicate time for, while Liberals were united on coercion, most were unenthusiastic about the Irish Land Law Bill currently before Parliament. In a stirring declamation appealing to Liberal susceptibilities, Parnell assured them that 'those who may have been inclined to turn to outrage or to turn to physical force or to methods outside of, and unknown to, the constitution have turned, in consequence of the admission of the people to the franchise, to constitutional methods'.[31] However, on 21 July Parnell offered conditional support for the Land Bill: 'I believe that if this measure, with the suggestions I have made, was passed and fairly worked it would be accepted by the tenants of Ireland as a satisfactory means of tiding them over their present difficulties.'[32] The following day the Irish Privy Council proclaimed 18 counties and partially proclaimed 13 others. Within the initial month proceedings under the Criminal Law and Procedure Act were taken against 659 persons. It was to prove a turning point, for thereafter the government held the initiative. By May 1889 25 MPs and a number of priests were sentenced to prison.

On 19 August the National League was proclaimed as a 'dangerous association'. Four days afterwards the Land Act was passed; it admitted about 100,000 leaseholders to the Land Act of 1881, allowed tenants threatened with eviction because of inability to pay excessive rents to apply to the courts for reductions in proportion to commodity prices falls, and empowered the land courts to revise judicial rents fixed before 1886. Although the legislation did not 'solve' the problem or meet all of Parnell's points, it removed an immediate rationale for Parnell's active involvement in the Plan of Campaign, while the Criminal Law and Procedure Act would undoubtedly have been implemented against him if he had spoken in favour of the Plan in Ireland. The land measure had a substantial impact on lowering the numbers of evictions, thereby weakening the appeal of the Plan.

The land question was not ended by the new act. In an attempt to push the issue, Archbishop Walsh, in a letter to the *Freeman's Journal*, published on 29 August, proposed a Round Table Conference of representatives of landlords and tenants to work out an agreement.[33] Walsh's intervention soon languished but whetted his appetite for meddling; he persisted through the autumn to resuscitate the conference in an ill-disguised attempt to supplant the secular leadership.

Balfour's combination of measures proved effective. In November Salisbury claimed that conditions in Ireland were improving. Parnell himself was sidelined by illness through most of the autumn. By the close of the year the numbers of local branches of the National League nose-dived, its funds were diminishing, suppressed branches met only at irregular intervals and their edicts were less virulent than in the past. The Plan of Campaign depended on the energy of a few men, particularly O'Brien and Dillon. Imprisonment of one or both tended to cause the agitation to subside.

During 1888 Parnell spoke in public only twice, but this belies the extent of his political presence as he pursued a consistently active role in the House of Commons. In the early months of the session he spoke on numerous Irish topics and was present, when well, in divisions. The political position was sharply affected by a circular from the Vatican on 20 April, condemning the Plan on three grounds – it was unlawful to break contracts freely accepted by landlord and tenant; rental levels could be adjudicated in land courts; and monies collected were extorted from tenants. Boycotting was denounced. Geary asserts that the Papal Rescript was generally ignored by priests already supporting the Plan.[34] His judgement underestimates the psychological value of its impact.[35]

Parnell's speech at the National Liberal Club on 8 May 1888 attracted acute interest and has been analysed closely. It was delivered not merely in the wake of the Rescript, but also immediately after O'Brien had received a three-month prison sentence on the 4th and Dillon's certainty of imprisonment (he received six months on the 9th). He insisted that the Papal Rescript was a matter for Catholics, not Protestants like himself. He distanced himself from the agitation, stating that due to his absence from political life through illness 'I knew nothing about the Plan of Campaign until weeks after it had been started.'[36] He praised its effectiveness but said that, had he been asked, he would have counselled against its adoption. Due to the prosecutions of Dillon and O'Brien, he could not abort the Plan but laid down conditions – the National League and Irish Party should not be identified with it; the sphere of operation should be restricted to estates where it already existed; and there should be moderation in speech and action. He defended 'the right of combination, the right of free speech, freedom of the press and of public meetings as necessary for the securing of our liberties in Ireland'.

Parnell indirectly returned to the agrarian agitation in his only other speech that year on 13 June. While praising the courage of those who had been imprisoned and attacking coercion he virtually ignored the Plan. Instead he chose to emphasise that as a conse-quence of franchise extension the National League was the 'first constitutional movement in our time which have really rested upon the people at their base'.[37] He maintained that 'it has brought the people into intimate association with constitutional ideas, it has shown them the value of their votes, the power of constitutional means, and the enormous importance and advantages in these days of Parliamentary methods – of Parliamentary methods supported by intelligent agitating organisation and co-operation from the people of Ireland'. Adherence to this path, he argued, had aligned the British people with Ireland and an election which must come soon would return Gladstone to power.

Meanwhile, F. H. O'Donnell's failed action against *The Times* [O'Donnell *v.* Walter] on 5 July brought Parnellism and crime to the forefront again. On 9 July Parnell requested a Select Committee 'for the purpose of inquiring into the authenticity of the letters read at the recent trial, containing serious charges against myself and several other Members of this House'.[38] This would mark the commencement of the fifth seminal episode of Parnell's career. The government, sensing that it had the ammunition to discredit the nationalists, on 17 July introduced a bill to establish a special commission to inquire into all charges made against Irish MPs and others. The Special Commission Act was passed on 13 August.

In the House of Commons on 23 July 1888 Parnell claimed credit for converting the Irish people away from extremism. He sought 'to teach them to value parliamentary methods and the safety of entrance within the gates of the Constitution'.[39] Improved conditions in Ireland Balfour attributed to the Crimes Act, Papal Rescript, and a good harvest. By December there were only 130 cases of boycotting. This was a remarkable turnaround from the 4,835 on 31 July 1887 or even the 2,469 at the end of that year.

SPECIAL COMMISSION TO THE DIVORCE COURT VERDICT

The Special Commission sat from 17 September 1888 to 22 November 1889, holding 129 sessions. Its terms of reference were loaded against the Irish Party while the financial cost was a heavy burden. Parnell eschewed speaking in public until after Richard Pigott's dramatic exposure in February 1889 as the forger of the letters published in *The Times*. As well, Parnell's participation in the House of Commons during the autumn session ebbed. Ultimately, the proceedings and conclusions of the Commission were open to just about whatever polemical interpretation fitted pre-conceived opinions but, so far as nationalist and Liberal opinion was concerned, Parnell had been vindicated. He made good use of his advantage.

On 8 March 1889 at the '80 Club, Parnell reiterated the primacy of the Liberal alliance and the value of working within the constitution. He suggested that the legislation passed by Gladstone since 1869 'prepared the way for the great triumph of constitutional principles in Ireland'.[40] For Parnell, working within the constitution was not an end in itself but a means to achieve what the people needed. In late May, in the wake of testifying before the

Special Commission, he pointed out that parliamentarianism was on trial; it was incumbent upon MPs to gain the respect of Ireland's people by securing those things the nation demanded.[41]

Finally, in summer of 1889, Parnell gave half-hearted support to the failing land movement. When a new Tenants' Defence Association was formally launched in Thurles, County Tipperary, on 28 October, he did not attend but wrote to the Lord Mayor outlining its very limited objects: 'to protect tenants against the landlord conspiracy, uphold civil liberties, [and] assert basic trade union rights of combination'.[42] He remained unwilling to allow diversions that might undermine his parliamentary work.

At the close of 1889, at Nottingham en route to staying with Gladstone at Hawarden for discussions on the future Home Rule Bill, Parnell commented on the underlying objective of self-government which was to bring prosperity to Ireland. He also proclaimed that the Liberals 'have given them confidence in the ways of the Constitution'.[43] After meeting Gladstone, he admonished critics of constitutionalism in a speech at Liverpool, 'it would be madness for them to talk of physical force or to turn from the ways of the Constitution to the ways of rebellion and of treason'.[44] 'Past rebellions', he proclaimed, 'had been partially justified 'by neglect of the Parliament of England to attend to their wants.'

At the close of the year the political world was abuzz with Captain O'Shea's divorce petition naming Parnell as co-respondent. While uncertainty filled the air, no one considered it to be the unmaking of The Chief's leadership. First, the relationship with Mrs O'Shea was widely known. Second, such arrangements were not unusual: Hartington lived with the Duchess of Manchester; Butt's private life had caused little stir. The moral climate had shifted, although Parnell's immense status appeared unshakeable. At a dinner in his honour on 28 June 1890 he warned:

If the Constitution is forbidden to us, it will not be our fault if constitutional methods have failed. We shall have tried and we should then give place to other men. Whether you should take part in such things, or whether I should take part in such things I know not, but this I do know – that we have honestly trodden the paths of the Constitution . . . we do believe that Ireland can be saved within the Constitution.[45]

His stress on the constitution had become a mainspring of post-1886 ideology.

CONCLUSION

After mid-1882 Parnell's position was to focus on affairs in Parliament; popular opinion had the role of strengthening his hand at Westminster. Like Butt, he always appreciated the essential link between parliamentarianism and public opinion – that Parliament must be informed of Irish wants and the people at home taught what they could legitimately expect from Westminster. Before 1880 Parnell had participated in a wide range of debates; afterwards he concentrated his energies on Irish matters. Gladstone's Home Rule proposal, however, brought a shake of the kaleidoscope. Parnell's capacity to make and sustain ministries, briefly exercised in 1885–6, was neutered, and thereafter he could effectively influence legislation only in conjunction with Liberals. This was a facsimile of Butt's situation in 1874, though Parnell had of course established a firmer grip on Catholic affection, led a stronger party, and exerted more compelling influence on Liberalism.

CHAPTER 9

The Split
November 1890–October 1891

THE DIVORCE

On 15 November 1890 Captain O'Shea's petition was heard. For reasons that remain a mystery, it was not defended. Captain O'Shea told a lurid tale of deceit by Parnell and his wife. Two days later he was granted a *decree nisi*. Initially the outcome was greeted calmly, but anti-Parnell feeling swiftly materialised. Parnell's last campaign with its destructive legacy for the hopes of Home Rule and his appeal to the 'hillside men' or revolutionary forces seems at odds with his attachment to constitutional and parliamentary traditions. In recent analyses of this controversial episode, both Philip Bull and Frank Callanan – from opposite perspectives – stress his continuity of outlook. Bull alleges that Parnell's commitment to parliamentarianism was always conditional; Callanan maintains that he remained fundamentally a constitutionalist during the final struggle.[1] At the end of this phase of his career Parnell continued to see public opinion as the means to restore his parliamentary authority.

Parnell's post-divorce-court actions went through several stages: the maintenance of normality, 17–28 November; indecision, 29 November to 1 December; squabble between parliamentarians, 1–6 December; initial struggle for public opinion, 7–29 December; Boulogne negotiations, 30 December 1890 to 11 February 1891; and Parnell's search for new bases of support, 11 January to 6

October. Throughout these months Parnell campaigned more widely in Ireland than at any previous time. It had been a decade since he had appeared regularly on Irish platforms. Parnell articulated seven broad themes:

- his leadership was derived from the people, not the party, and he could only be deposed by the nation;
- he alone could vouchsafe a satisfactory Home Rule measure;
- he demanded complete independence from English parties;
- he criticised clerical influence in politics;
- the land question was critically appraised;
- he proposed a programme of reforms in addition to self-government;
- His personal life was a private not a political matter.

The campaign highlighted important aspects of Parnell's relationship with the 'nation'; on the other side of the ledger the opposition sought the de-legitimisation of his authority. In particular the episode highlighted that

- Parnell's lack of concerted interest in organisational matters left him vulnerable;
- Newspaper support proved unreliable, thus limiting a usual avenue of communication and influence;
- *Mores* had shifted, cutting Parnell adrift, notably from the 'organic intelligentsia' or democracy from below.

Support for a wider social reform agenda marked a new departure. In the past, when faced with dissent, Parnell had emphasised the great single issue of Home Rule; now, when opponents decreed that only by rejecting him could self-government be salvaged, he laid claim to an expanded mission. In his public speeches he reviewed his and the opposition's parliamentary records, a reminder of the centrality of the House of Commons in this bitter contest. Also, his political and economic positions during the campaign warrant close attention. Callanan draws attention to his pronouncements on land purchase, vision on other economic issues, championship of an interventionist policy to foster industry and rural development in a home rule state as well as pointing out Parnell's challenge to the configuration of power within Irish society and his attempt to recast the nationalist polity.[2] The scene was set in Parnell's first public address, on 10 December 1890 in Dublin, where he stated: 'I have claimed that the integrity and independence of the Irish Party must be beyond things and above all things.'[3]

PARTY SPLIT

On 25 November 1890 Parnell was re-elected chairman of the Irish Party for the coming parliamentary session. Opposition against his leadership quickly mounted. Gladstone demanded Parnell's withdrawal. Parnell responded, publishing on 29 November a manifesto 'To the People of Ireland' to uphold his leadership. A number of Irish Party MPs requisitioned a party meeting to reconsider Parnell's position. This acrimonious gathering met between 1 and 6 December in Committee Room 15 of the House of Commons. On 3 December, in the midst of the proceedings, the standing committee of the Catholic hierarchy denounced Parnell. On the 6th, Justin McCarthy, vice-chairman of the party, and a majority of MPs withdrew and met as a separate group soon to be known as anti-Parnellites. The party split was reality, but the country had yet to be heard. The legend of Parnell, torn from his pinnacle by Liberal wirepullers, treacherous colleagues and priests was in the making.

In the immediate aftermath of the division of the party Parnell sought to defend his political record and mitigate the effects of the divorce. On 10 December in Dublin he pointed to his ill health and declared 'my defence will be known some day', while identifying himself with the aspirations of rural labourers and urban working-men.[4] In Cork, where Parnell had gone to meet his constituents before travelling on to campaign in the by-election in Kilkenny North, Parnell devoted one of his speeches to the interests of the workers, declaring he would do all he could for them; he received the endorsement of a secretary of the Cork Labour Federation who pledged the support of nine-tenths of the labourers of Ireland.[5] At a meeting immediately afterwards Parnell declared support for agricultural labourers and reiterated his identity with the quest of industrial worker: 'my thoughts and my instincts have always been directed to the workingmen of Ireland as the future safety and the future hope of our nation'. He went on to insist they were the build-ing blocks of Ireland. Callanan suggests that from the Rotunda speech onwards he sought to co-opt the allegiance of the Fenian tradition, labouring classes, and the youth of the country against the tenant farmers, who he suspected were amenable to priestly influence.[6]

The first test of opinion in the country was close to hand – the parliamentary by-election for Kilkenny North, a primarily rural constituency. Parnell campaigned vigorously, speaking to numerous audiences until announcement of the poll on 23 December. His main theme was that his opponents succumbed to Liberal dictation. Many expected Parnell to triumph but, as Callanan shows, Healy's developing rhetoric of Parnell as an anachronism and Davitt's zealous organisation centring on the 'organic intelligentsia' carried the day with the anti-Parnellite coasting to victory (2,527– 1,362). During the campaign he proclaimed on 13 December that 'I will allow no combination, however strong, however influential, however apparently respectable, to drive me from my duty to Ireland. While I have life I will go from one constituency to another, from one county to another, from one city to another, from one town and village and parish to another, to put what I know is the truth before the people . . . To the voice of Ireland alone will I bow.'[7]

SEARCH FOR SUPPORT

On 30 December, Parnell, O'Brien and Dillon met in Boulogne about the leadership; negotiations lasted into early February. The respective purposes of the two sides were incompatible. For O'Brien and Dillon the motivation was to find a means to ease Parnell's path into retirement and bring about political reunion; for Parnell the object was to demonstrate to supporters anxious about the split that he was open to reasonable compromise. At Limerick on 11 January Parnell began a fresh series of public defences of his leadership. He stated that with amendments, notably compulsory purchase, the Tory Land Bill of the last session provided grounds for the solution to the land question whereas Liberals under Radical influence had given up on tenant land purchase.[8] At Tralee on 18 January Parnell stated that he had refused to oppose Balfour's light railway scheme because it would bring benefits to the west and return some of the money from the over-taxation of Ireland.[9] He would repeat this contention at Galway on 15 March.[10] On 23 January he said: 'I am as willing as I was then [1870s] to go into the lobby as one Irishman against 650 Englishmen.'[11] At Waterford City on 25 January he again expressed a desire to improve the condition of the working classes and less well-off.[12] He also expressed his aspiration, 'I hope for all classes that the day will soon come when Irishmen may feel that under the fostering care of a native Legislature they have a free field before them for that great and bright genius of head and of hand and of heart which has so distinguished our people in every field throughout the world over.'

His position was to stress the value of the constitutional approach, as he did at Longford on 23 February, where he reminded Irishmen:

> I am a constitutional leader, and believe that the constitutional forces which we have at our command are sufficient for the settlement of this question. Believing that, I shall stand upon this constitutional platform until they have torn away the last plank from under our feet. I can say that during my 16 years of public life I have never, whether in secret thought, or public act or word, tampered with the national aspirations of Ireland, or sought to prevent stronger, abler, or more courageous men than I am from pressing forward. I desire to say here tonight that I believe we can win on the constitutional platform; but, if we cannot win upon it, well, I shall be prepared to give way to better and stronger men, and it can never be said of us that, by anything that we have done, we have prevented better or abler men than ourselves from dealing with the future of our race.[13]

Parnell's speech at Clerkenwell on 4 March, where he endorsed the cause of British working men, is significant. He expressed disbelief in industrial action and cited the role of Parliament in the resolution of grievances. Parnell saw workers engaged in an 'unequal struggle against capital and against his employer'.[14]

At Newry on 8 March, Parnell conceded that next election would not produce an untrammelled outcome: 'although we may not have as numerous a party as we had in 1885, it will be more solid, it will be stronger, its principles will be clearer, sharper, and more independent; and that with such a party we shall secure the respect of the English people and of the nations of the world'.[15] Considering this and other aspects of the search for a base of support, Callanan argues, 'Parnell's claim to have rallied a cohesive and purposeful minority had . . . considerable substance. He had assembled a formidable minoritarian coalition which was less factious and disparate than anti-Parnellite rhetoricians could afford to concede.' 'If Parnellism was by the time of the later split distinctly a minority allegiance', he adds, 'and likely to remain so indefinitely, it possessed a sociological as well as a political coherence which posed a serious challenge to the pretensions of anti-Parnellite nationalism.'[16]

On 14 March in Dublin Parnell put the rise of labour in the context of representation and the constitution:

> The power which the Constitution gives to the masses – the political power which it gives – the power which it gives them of influencing the election and of using their force for returning members of Parliament, it is a growing and an increasing one, and all of us politicians are bound to recognise it, and even if we do not sympathise with you we must now sympathise with you in order to maintain our political existence.[17]

He promised to do all he could for the urban working classes by legislative means, 'whether in the Parliament of Westminster or the Parliament of College Green'. Parnell's concept of independence was based on the same premise. At Cork city on 17 March he reminded his audience that it was never intended that an Irish party should devote itself to working permanently through parliamentary channels if it failed to represent the people and gain results. Additionally, he professed, 'Ireland without trade, without industry, but merely as an agricultural country, never can be a nation.'[18] A nation without trade and industry would be 'maimed and incomplete'.

The Sligo North parliamentary by-election posed a further test of the relative strengths of Parnellites and anti-Parnellites, albeit in a rural constituency where the influence of the clergy was profound. There again Parnell expressed support for the poorer classes. He maintained that only a completely independent party could serve Irish needs. There he repeatedly lent support to Balfour's Land Bill which aimed to expand tenant purchase. On 25 March Parnell proposed to reduce the numbers of the Irish Constabulary by a third over six years, thereby generating large financial savings which he would give to landlords enabling them to let 250,000 small tenants go rent free in perpetuity. It was, he said, 'not a wild scheme; it is one that I have thought over for many years'.[19] At the same time he urged reduction of rents by 30 per cent on larger holdings, facilitating tenant purchase. He proposed loaning money to landlords at an easy rate of interest, enabling encumbered landowners to pay off debts. When the ballots were counted on 2 April the anti-Parnellite won (3,261–2,493).

On 5 April he was back on the campaign trail, speaking at an Amnesty Association rally in Phoenix Park, Dublin. Parnell decreed, 'Liberals had always been distinguished for making political prisoners and the Tories for letting them out of prison, and while the Liberals had pelted the Irish people with hailstones the Tories had sometimes given them some of the gentle rain from heaven.'[20] His support for Balfour's Land Bill was unabated. It was, he observed in the House of Commons on 16 April, something the tenants themselves wanted.[21] In numerous speeches he drew a distinction between his own attitude and the unrepresentative rejection of the measure by the anti-Parnellites, accusing them of surrendering to the blandishments of Liberals and Radicals rather than advancing the wants of the Irish people. At Irishtown, County Mayo, on 19 April he denounced the successionists who had voted against provisions of the Land Bill that would reduce rents.

I have always believed that by making the Irish tenant-farmer prosperous and independent of his landlord, by reducing his rent, by giving him and the labourers something to put in their bellies, we were not diminishing the forces of Irish nationality, but increasing them. . . . we are told that Ireland is to be a nation of one religion only . . . The Nationalists of Ireland . . .will sacrifice everything, will face every intimidation, in order to secure that our Irish nation is to be the nation of our people. We cannot spare one single Irishman. We welcome within our ranks all religious, believing that only so can we have a united Ireland, and prove once more the title of our country to nationhood.[22]

At Clonmel on 26 April he again supported the aspirations of the workers.[23] The next day in Clonmel he praised Tipperary's readiness in the past to resort to extra-constitutional methods to protect its needs, but 'as an apostle of constitutional methods' he would be ashamed should this ever be required again.[24] When speaking at Kilcock, County Kildare, on 10 May Parnell defended the idea of having two parties representative of the national interest; this was typical elsewhere in democratic states. He also declared: 'I would rather be the leader of a good minority than of a rotten majority.'[25]

At Maryborough on 17 May he supported the beneficial effects of the Land Bill for tenant purchase and then on arrival in Belfast on 22 May Parnell praised the Land Bill: 'I am perfectly willing to take whatever benefits and concessions for my countrymen that I can obtain from any government, I care not whether Whig or Tory.'[26] Furthermore, in Belfast he supported the claims of labour when it made reasonable proposals and pointed to the power of the parliamentary weapon. At Wicklow Town on 31 May Parnell expanded on his chief themes: 'I always have been convinced that with the extension of the suffrage which we obtained in 1885, and with the cordial acceptance by the Irish people of that suffrage as a means for enabling them to wield the constitutional weapon with effect, that all things would come to Ireland.'[27] He maintained the urgency of encouraging industry, protecting tenant farmers, keeping the population at home, and supplying employment to labourers. At Inchicore, where he addressed a rally on 7 June, he repeated, 'I am anxious that everything should be done, both legislatively and by combination, to improve the lot of workers.'[28] He supported their endeavours to secure political representation. Independence was essential, he told an audience at Bermondsey on 17 June. The just passed Land Bill 'if properly worked by the Land Commission and by the Irish Government, would do more good to Ireland and its people than any measure that had every proceeded from the Imperial Parliament'.[29]

Meanwhile, on 25 June, Katharine O'Shea and Parnell married. This further undermined morale and his support in Ireland. Still, he had to fight on in the Carlow parliamentary by-election, another predominantly rural constituency. 'It was of great importance', he said on 29 June, 'that the people of Ireland should believe that they can gain their rights by sending independent members into Westminster.'[30] The anti-Parnell candidate won handily on 8 July (3,755–1,539). In its wake, Dillon and O'Brien took sides against Parnell and the *Freeman's Journal* shortly thereafter abandoned his ranks. Yet, as Callanan notes, his electoral decline had probably bottomed out.[31]

On 18 July at Newcastle-under-Lyme, Parnell gave further emphasis to the weapon in the hands of working men: 'The labour question will be, after the Irish question, the greatest question of the future and to the men who work with their hands will belong, if they intelligently use the constitutional power which is now theirs, will belong the direction of the political future of this country.'[32] He inserted compulsory land purchase in the platform of the National Convention which met on 23 July.[33]

In his final speech at Creggs, County Roscommon, on 27 September Parnell promised to continue to fight to maintain independence.[34]

DEATH

On 6 October Parnell died in Brighton. It was as though he had fashioned his own epitaph during the Kilkenny by-election the previous December:

> The gates of darkness are open before us, and we are even now walking in the valley of the shadow of death; yet the light will surely come. The light of the Irish sunburst, which has never been obscured, and which never will, but will always be a beacon to our nation, will encourage us forward, will lighten our path, will show us the true road, and on the true road we will walk together to victory.[35]

It was now, as William O'Brien later remarked, that 'one-man power was replaced for Ireland by eighty-man powerless'.[36]

Parnell's career had many elements, not all of them ideally consistent. He made a significant contribution to the discussion of the Irish economy, on the functions of self-government, about political organisation, the utility of parliamentary representation and the social structure of his island. His life is useful for testing and modifying theoretical models.

Parnell's contribution went beyond the exigencies of Irish nationalism. He pioneered methods that brought the events of the 'alien' parliament at Westminster to every hearth in Ireland and additionally forced British opinion 'to hear what otherwise we should not'.

Parnell deserves to be remembered as an exemplar of Bagehot's constitution. His career tells much about the parameters of Irish nationalism in the later Victorian era, but also illustrates practically the appeal and relevance of the English constitution. George Boyce neatly sums up Parnell's place in parliamentary history:

> It is not the least of the many paradoxes of Parnell's career that, through his placing of Irish Home Rule firmly on the parliamentary agenda, he should have ended up delaying the transformation of parliament from the assembly celebrated by Walter Bagehot to the legislative factory that it was, after 1918, to become. In a real sense, then, Parnell was one of the last great figures of the Victorian Constitution, with its unshaken belief in the resolution of political conflict through parliamentary means . . . If it did nothing else, the rise and fall of Parnell preserved the raison d'être of the British parliament. Bagehot made possible Parnell; and Parnell give a significant, if in the end illusory, extension to the life of Bagehot.[37]

Notes

Chapter 1: *The Makings of a Nationalist*

1 Reinhard Bendix, *Max Weber: An Intellectual Portrait* (London, 1960), pp. 297–304.

2 R. F. Foster, *Charles Stewart Parnell: The Man and his Family* (Hassocks, 1976), pp. 16–29.

3 Ibid., pp. 150–1.

4 *The Times*, 28 June 1886.

5 Ged Martin, 'Parnell at Cambridge: the education of an Irish nationalist', *Irish Historical Studies* 19 (Mar. 1974), pp. 72–82; *The Times Higher Education Supplement*, 20 May 1994.

6 Quoted in Foster, *Parnell*, pp. 132–3.

7 Oliver P. Rafferty, *The Church, The State and the Fenian Threat 1861–75* (Basingstoke and London, 1999), p. 145.

8 Foster, *Charles Stewart Parnell*, pp. xii–xx; idem, *Paddy and Mr Punch: Connections in Irish and English History* (London, 1993), pp. 48–61.

9 Paul Bew, *Enigma: A New Life of Charles Stewart Parnell* (Dublin, 2011), p. 23.

10 Tony Claydon, 'The political thought of Charles Stewart Parnell' in D. George Boyce and Alan O'Day (eds), *Parnell in Perspective* (London and New York, 1991), pp. 151–71.

11 Frank Callanan, *The Parnell Split, 1890–91* (Cork, 1992), p. 299.

12 Miroslav Hroch, *Social Preconditions of National Revival in Europe* (Cambridge, 1985), pp. 172–4.

13 See Michael Hechter, *Internal Colonialism: The Celtic Fringe in British National Development 1536–1966* (Berkeley, CA and London, 1975).

14 Liam Kennedy, 'The economic thought of the nation's lost leader: Charles Stewart Parnell' in Boyce and O'Day (eds), *Parnell in Perspective*, pp. 171–200.

15 Callanan, *The Parnell Split*, p. 290.
16 Ibid., p. 281.

Chapter 2: *Political Apprentice, 1874–6*

1 Bendix, *Max Weber*, pp. 297–8.
2 Hroch, *Social Preconditions*, pp. 134, 161–2, 183, 185–6.
3 Foster, *Charles Stewart Parnell*, pp. 190–6.
4 *Freeman's Journal*, 11 Mar. 1874.
5 See, Clive Dewey, 'Celtic agrarian legislation and the Celtic revival: historicist implications of Gladstone's Irish and Scottish Land Acts, 1870–1886', *Past & Present*, 64 (1974), pp. 30–70; *Freeman's Journal*, 22 Jan. 1875.
6 *Freeman's Journal*, 23 Jan. 1875.
7 *Drogheda Argus*, 17 Apr. 1875.
8 Quoted in Alan Ware, *Political Parties and Party Systems* (Oxford and New York, 1996), p. 5.
9 Peter Lassman and Ronald Speirs (eds), *Weber: Political Writings* (Cambridge, 1994), pp. 336–7.
10 *Nation*, 21 Feb. 1874.
11 *Hansard*, 3rd series, ccxviii, 136–7 (20 Mar. 1874).
12 *Nation*, 28 Mar. 1874.
13 Benedict Anderson, *Imagined Communities: Reflections on the Origin and Spread of Nationalism* (London, 1983), pp. 15, 47, 62.
14 Bernadette Lally, *Print Culture in Loughrea 1850–1900: Reading, Writing and Printing in an Irish Provincial Town* (Dublin and Portland, OR, 2008), p. 39.
15 Walter Bagehot, *The English Constitution* (17th edn, London, 1985), pp. 150–82.
16 *Hansard*, 3rd series, ccxxiii, 1643–5 (26 Apr. 1875).
17 Ibid., 3rd series, ccxxv, 1201–2 (8 July 1875).
18 Ibid., ccxxvi, 335 (31 July 1875).
19 *The People* (Wexford), 9 Oct. 1875.
20 *Nation*, 23 Oct. 1875.
21 *Freeman's Journal*, 19 Jan. 1876.
22 *Hansard*, 3rd series, ccxxvii, 1851 (10 Mar. 1876).
23 Ibid., ccxxviii, 1213–14 (4 Apr. 1876).
24 Ibid., ccxxix, 1399 (29 May 1876).
25 Ibid., ccxxx, 808 (30 June 1875).
26 *Nation*, 8 July 1876.

27 Hicks Beach to Disraeli, 20 July 1876 (Bodleian Library, Oxford, Beaconsfield Papers, Box 118).
28 *United Irishman*, 18 Nov. 1876.

Chapter 3: *Obstruction, 1877*

1 James Bryce, *Studies in Contemporary Biography* (London, 1903), pp. 241–2.
2 H. C. G. Matthew, 'Rhetoric and politics in Britain, 1860–1950' in P. J. Waller, *Politics and Social Change in Modern Britain* (Brighton, 1987), pp. 43, 48.
3 Lassman and Speirs (eds), *Weber*, pp. 318, 336–7, 342.
4 Sigmund Neumann, *Modern Political Parties* (Chicago, 1967), p. 405.
5 *Nation*, 10 Feb. 1877.
6 *Hansard*, 3rd series, ccxxxii, 348 (14 Feb. 1877).
7 Ibid., 1635 (8 Mar. 1877).
8 *Liverpool Mercury*, 21 Mar. 1877.
9 *Hansard*, 3rd series, ccxxxii, 528 (26 Mar. 1877).
10 Ibid., ccxxxiii, 1049 (12 Apr. 1877).
11 *Freeman's Journal*, 26 May 1877.
12 Ibid.
13 Hansard, 3rd series, ccxxxiv, 20 (1 May 1877).
14 Ibid., 178.
15 *Freeman's Journal*, 23 May 1877.
16 Ibid., 28 May 1877.
17 *Glasgow Herald*, 29 May 1877.
18 *Hansard*, 3rd series, ccxxxiv, 1596–7 (11 June 1877).
19 *The Times*, 20 June 1877.
20 *Liverpool Mercury*, 16 July 1877.
21 *Hansard*, 3rd series, ccxxxv, 1733 (23 July 1877).
22 Ibid., 1807 (25 July 1877).
23 Ibid., ccxxxvi, 129 (28 July 1877).
24 Ibid., 187 (30 July 1877).
25 *The Times*, 30 July 1877.
26 Ibid., 8 Aug. 1877.
27 Emmet Larkin, *The Roman Catholic Church and the Emergence of the Modern Irish Political System, 1874–1878* (Dublin, 1996), pp. 469–78.
28 *Ulster Examiner*, 29 Sept. 1877.
29 Ibid., 29 Sept. 1877.
30 *Nation*, 13 Oct. 1877.

31 Ibid., 15 Dec. 1877.
32 Bew, *Enigma*, pp. 38–9.

Chapter 4: *Activism and the Dawn of the Land Question*

1   *Nation*, 19 Jan. 1878.
2   *Hansard*, 3rd series, ccxxxvii, 196–7 (18 Jan. 1878).
3   Ibid., ccxxxviii, 521–2 (28 Feb. 1878).
4   Ibid., 592 (1 Mar. 1878).
5   Ibid., ccxxxix, 58 (26 Mar. 1878).
6   Ibid., 597 (4 Apr. 1878).
7   Ibid., 750 (5 Apr. 1878).
8   Ibid., 1414 (16 Apr. 1878).
9   Ibid., 1601–4 (9 May 1878).
10 Ibid., 1627 (9 May 1878).
11 Ibid., ccxl, 935–40 (30 May 1878).
12 Ibid., 1505 (14 June 1878).
13 *Nation*, 26 Oct. 1878.
14 *Nation*, 9 Nov. 1878.
15 Ibid., 23 Nov. 1878.
16 Ibid.
17 *Sunderland Daily Echo*, 14 Jan. 1879.
18 *Durham Chronicle*, 17 Jan. 1879.
19 *Newcastle Chronicle*, 17 Jan. 1879.
20 *Freeman's Journal*, 5 Feb. 1879.
21 Ibid., 11 Feb. 1879.
22 *Hansard*, 3rd series, ccxliii, 1156–7 (13 Feb. 1879).
23 Ibid., cccxliv, 479–81 (7 Mar. 1879).
24 *Freeman's Journal*, 15 Apr. 1879.
25 Ibid., 17 Apr. 1879.
26 *Hansard*, 3rd series, ccxlvi, 1397 (27 May 1879).

Chapter 5: *The Land War*

1   See James H. Murphy, *Abject Loyalty: Nationalism and Monarchy in Ireland During the Reign of Queen Victoria* (Washington, DC and Cork, 2001); James Loughlin, *The British Monarchy and Ireland: 1800 to the Present* (Cambridge and New York, 2007).

2   *Freeman's Journal*, 9 June 1879.

3   *Irish Times*, 2 Sept. 1879.

4   *Freeman's Journal*, 12 Sept. 1879.

5   *Nation*, 23 Sept. 1879.

6   Barbara Lewis Solow, *The Land Question and the Irish Economy, 1870–1903* (Cambridge, MA and London, 1971).

7   *Freeman's Journal*, 29 Sept. 1879.

8   Ibid., 12 Oct. 1879.

9   *Ulster Examiner*, 16 Oct. 1879.

10 Ibid., 18 Oct. 1879.

11 *Freeman's Journal*, 17 Nov. 1879.

12 Ibid., 24 Nov. 1879.

13 *New York Herald*, 3 Jan. 1880.

14 *Fall River Daily Herald*, 15 Jan. 1880; *New York Times*, 5 Jan. 1880.

15 *Congressional Record*, x, pt 1, pp. 664–5.

16 *Cincinnati Commercial*; *Cincinnati Gazette*; *Cincinnati Enquirer*, 21 Feb. 1880.

17 *Peoria National Democrat*, 3 Mar. 1880.

18 *Freeman's Journal*, 9 Apr. 1880.

19 Ibid., 15 Apr. 1880.

20 *The Times*, 20 Sept. 1880.

21 *Freeman's Journal*, 25 Oct. 1880.

22 Katharine O'Shea, *Charles Stewart Parnell: His Love Story and Political Life* (2 vols, London, 1914), II, pp. 207, 235–6.

23 Quoted in F. S. L. Lyons, *Charles Stewart Parnell* (London, 1997), p. 201.

Chapter 6: *Parliamentary Politics*

1   H. C. G. Matthew, *Gladstone, 1809–1898* (Oxford, 1998), p. 457.

2   Quoted in Lyons, *Parnell*, p. 202.

3   *Hansard*, 3rd series, cclxxi, 729–30 (28 June 1882).

4   K. Theodore Hoppen, 'Gladstone, Salisbury and the end of Irish assimilationism' in Mary E. Daly and K. Theodore Hoppen (eds), *Gladstone: Ireland and Beyond* (Dublin, 2011), pp. 45–63.

5   N. C. Fleming and Alan O'Day, 'Accommodation, conciliation and cooperation: a Gladstonian legacy' in D. George Boyce and Alan O'Day (eds), *Gladstone and Ireland: Politics, Religion and Nationality in the Victorian Age* (Basingstoke and New York, 2010), pp. 233–55.

6   *Freeman's Journal*, 17 Aug. 1882.

7   Ibid., 22 Aug. 1882.

8   Quoted in J. L. Hammond, *Gladstone and the Irish Nation* (London and New York, 1938), p. 308.

9   Lassman and Speirs (eds), *Weber*, p. 337.

10   William L. Feingold, *The Revolt of the Tenantry* (Boston, 1984), p. 164.

11   Virginia Crossman, *Politics, Pauperism and Power in Late Nineteenth-Century Ireland* (Manchester and New York, 2006), p. 175.

12   Ibid., pp. 46–7.

13   See Jim Mac Laughlin, *Reimaging the Nation-State: The Contested Terrains of Nation Building* (London, 2001).

14   See, Tom Garvin, *The Evolution of Irish Nationalist Politics* (New York and Dublin, 1981).

15   Quoted in Frank Callanan, *T. M. Healy* (Cork, 1996), p. 100.

16   *Freeman's Journal*, 18 Oct. 1882; see Alan O'Day, *Irish Home Rule, 1867–1921* (Manchester and New York, 1998), pp. 79–81.

17   *Hansard*, 3rd series, cclxxx, 420 (30 Nov. 1882).

18   *Freeman's Journal*, 30 Aug. 1883.

19   Ibid., 12 Dec. 1883.

20   *Hansard,* 3rd series, cclxxxiv, 1908–15 (25 Feb. 1884).

21   *Freeman's Journal*, 7 Apr. 1884.

22   *United Ireland*, 19 Apr. 1884.

Chapter 7: *Home Rule*

1   James Loughlin, *Gladstone, Home Rule and the Ulster Question* (Dublin: 1986), p. 43.

2   Quoted in Mark Tierney, *Croke of Cashel: The Life of Archbishop Thomas William Croke, 1821–1902* (Dublin, 1976), p. 172.

3   C. H. D. Howard (ed.), 'Documents relating to the Irish "Central Board" scheme, 1884–5', *Irish Historical Studies* VIII: 31 (Mar. 1953), p. 242.

4   *Freeman's Journal*, 9 Jan. 1885.

5   *The Times*, 22 Jan. 1885.

6   Stephen Ball (ed.), *Dublin Castle and the First Home Rule Crisis: The Political Journal of Sir George Fottrell, 1884–1887* (London, 2008), p.13.

7   *Freeman's Journal*, 17 Aug. 1885.

8   Ibid., 21 Aug. 1885.

9   Ibid., 24 Aug. 1885.

10   Ibid., 25 Aug. 1885.

11   Ibid., 6 Oct. 1885.

12 Ibid., 30 Oct. 1885.

13 Ibid., 12 Oct. 1885.

14 Quoted in John Morley, *The Life of William Ewart Gladstone* (3 vols, London, 1903), III, p. 292.

15 *Hansard*, 3rd series, ccciv, 1036–85 (8 Apr. 1886).

16 Vernon Bogdanor, *Devolution* (Oxford, 1979).

17 *Hansard*, 3rd series, ccciv, 1124–34 (8 Apr. 1886).

18 *Hansard*, 3rd series, cccvi, 1175, 1179–80 (7 June 1886).

19 Crossman, *Politics, Law and Order in Nineteenth-Century Ireland* (Dublin, 1996), p. 154.

20 Murphy, *Abject Loyalty*, p. 252.

21 Reinhard Bendix, *Nation-Building and Citizenship* (Berkeley and Los Angeles, 1964), pp. 86–7.

Chapter 8: *The Plan of Campaign and the Conservatives*

1 *The Times*, 19 June 1886.

2 Ibid., 21 June 1886.

3 Ibid., 28 June 1886.

4 Ibid., 30 June 1886.

5 Ibid., 1 July 1886.

6 Ibid., 5 July 1886.

7 Henry Labouchere to Sir William Harcourt, 11 July 1886, Harcourt Papers (Bodleian Library, Oxford MS 57).

8 Quoted in Lady Victoria Hicks Beach, *The Life of Sir Michael Hicks Beach* (2 vols, London, 1932), I, p. 280.

9 Hicks Beach to Salisbury (copy), 25 July 1886, PCC/31 (St Aldwyn Papers, Gloucestershire Record Office).

10 *Freeman's Journal*, 16 Aug. 1886.

11 *Hansard*, 3rd series, cccviii, 59–70 (19 Aug. 1886).

12 Ibid., 291 (23 Aug. 1886).

13 Ibid., 311–13 (24 Aug. 1886)

14 Quoted in C. C. O'Brien, *Parnell and His Party, 1880–90* (corrected impression, Oxford, 1964), p. 200.

15 *Freeman's Journal*, 9 Sept. 1886.

16 Ibid., 11 Sept. 1886.

17 *United Ireland*, 23 Oct. 1886.

18 Laurence Geary, *The Plan of Campaign, 1886–1891* (Cork, 1986), p. 26.

19 Morley, *Life of Gladstone*, III, p. 281.

20 See Michael Hurst, *Joseph Chamberlain and the Liberal Reunion* (London and Toronto, 1967).

21 William O'Brien, *Evening Memories, Being a Continuation of Recollections* (London, 1920), pp. 177–83.

22 Hansard, 3rd series, cccx, 784, 789 (7 Feb. 1887).

23 Ibid., 794–9 (17 Feb. 1887).

24 L. P. Curtis, jr, *Coercion and Conciliation in Ireland, 1880–92: A Study in Conservative Unionism* (Princeton, NJ and London, 1963), p. 341.

25 See ibid.

26 Virginia Crossman, *Politics, Law and Order*, p. 162.

27 Catherine B. Shannon, *Arthur J. Balfour and Ireland 1874–1922* (Washington, DC, 1988), p. 45.

28 Andrew Gailey, *Ireland and the Death of Kindness: The Experience of Constructive Unionism, 1890–1905* (Cork, 1987); O'Callaghan, *British High Politics*, pp. 119–21.

29 *The Times*, 18 Mar. 1887.

30 *Hansard*, 3rd series, cccxxviii, 1225–32 (18 Apr. 1887).

31 *The Times*, 21 July 1887.

32 *Hansard*, 3rd series, cccxvii, 1711–14 (21 July 1887).

33 *Freeman's Journal*, 29 Aug. 1887.

34 Geary, *Plan of Campaign*, pp. 87–8.

35 Joseph V. O'Brien, *William O'Brien and the Course of Irish Politics, 1881–1918* (Berkeley, Los Angeles and London, 1976), p. 65.

36 *Freeman's Journal*, 9 May 1888.

37 Ibid., 14 June 1888.

38 Hansard, 3rd series, cccxxviii, 743 (9 July 1888).

39 Ibid., cccxxix, 252 (23 July 1888).

40 *The Times*, 9 March 1889.

41 *United Ireland*, 1 June 1889.

42 *Freeman's Journal*, 29 Oct. 1889.

43 *The Times*, 18 Dec. 1889.

44 Ibid., 20 Dec. 1889.

45 Ibid., 30 June 1890.

Chapter 9: *The Split*

1 Philip Bull, 'The fall of Parnell: the political context of his intransigence', in Boyce and O'Day (eds), *Parnell in Perspective*, pp. 129–47; Callanan, *The Parnell Split, 1890–91* (Cork, 1992).

2   Callanan, *Parnell Split*, pp. 276, 279, 20, 302.

3   *The Times*, 11 Dec. 1890.

4   Ibid.

5   *Freeman's Journal*, 12 Dec. 1890.

6   Callanan, *Parnell Split*, p. 277.

7   *United Ireland*, 27 Dec. 1890

8   *Freeman's Journal*, 12 Jan. 1891.

9   Ibid., 19 Jan. 1891.

10 *The Times*, 16 Mar. 1891.

11 *Freeman's Journal*, 16 Jan. 1891.

12 Ibid., 26 Jan. 1891.

13 Ibid., 24 Feb. 1891.

14 *The Times*, 5 Mar. 1891.

15 *Freeman's Journal*, 9 Mar. 1891.

16 Callanan, *Parnell Split*, p. 278.

17 *Freeman's Journal*, 16 Mar. 1891.

18 Ibid., 8 Mar. 1891; Callanan, *Parnell Split*, p. 290.

19 *Freeman's Journal*, 26 Mar. 1891.

20 *The Times*, 6 Apr. 1891.

21 *Hansard*, 3rd series, cclii, 1769–73 (16 Apr. 1891).

22 *Freeman's Journal*, 20 Apr. 1891.

23 Ibid., 27 Apr. 1891.

24 Ibid., 28 Apr. 1891.

25 Ibid., 27 Apr. 1891.

26 Ibid., 18, 22 May 1891.

27 Ibid., 1 June 1891.

28 Ibid., 8 June 1891.

29 *The Times*, 18 June 1891.

30 *Freeman's Journal*, 30 June 1891.

31 Callanan, *Parnell Split*, p. 170.

32 *Freeman's Journal*, 20 July 1891.

33 Ibid., 24 July 1891.

34 *United Ireland*, 3 Oct. 1891.

35 Ibid., 27 Dec. 1890.

36 William O'Brien, *An Olive Branch in Ireland and its History* (London, 1910), p. 67.

37 D. George Boyce, 'Parnell and Bagehot' in Boyce and O'Day (eds), *Parnell in Perspective*, p. 126.

Select Bibliography

The best source for literature on Parnell and his era is N. C. Fleming and Alan O'Day, *Charles Stewart Parnell and His Times: A Bibliography* (Santa Barbara, CA, 2011). R. Barry O'Brien, *The Life of Charles Stewart Parnell* (2 vols, London, edns 1898–1969) justly retains its place as a classic. F. S. L. Lyons, *Charles Stewart Parnell* (London, edns 1977–2005) is lengthy but not ageing gracefully, Robert Kee, *The Laurel and the Ivy: The Story of Charles Stewart Parnell and Irish Nationalism* (London, edns 1993–4) are valuable modern biographies, though the best source now is Paul Bew, *Enigma: A New Life of Charles Stewart Parnell* (Dublin, 2011), a new version of *Charles Stewart Parnell* (Dublin, edns 1980–91). Donal McCartney and Pauric Travers, *The Ivy Leaf: The Parnells Remembered* (Dublin, 2006) is an arresting and original set of essays about Parnell and his family. Two volumes marking the centenary of his death are D. George Boyce and Alan O'Day (eds), *Parnell in Perspective* (London, 1991) and Donal McCartney (ed.), *Parnell: The Politics of Power* (Dublin, 1991). Other useful modern works include R. F. Foster, *Charles Stewart Parnell: The Man and his Family* (Hassocks, edns 1976–9) and *Paddy and Mr Punch: Connections in Irish and English History* (London, edns 1993–95), William Michael Murphy, *The Parnell Myth and Irish Politics, 1891–1956* (New York, 1986), F. S. L. Lyons, *The Fall of Parnell, 1890–91* (London, edns 1960–2), Frank Callanan, *The Parnell Split, 1890–91* (Cork, 1992) and *T M. Healy* (Cork, 1996) and Michael Hurst, *Parnell and Irish Nationalism* (London, 1969). Special studies include Margery Brady, *The Love Story of Parnell and Katharine O'Shea* (Dublin, 1991), Jane McL. Côté, *Fanny and Anna Parnell: Ireland's Patriot Sisters* (London, 1991), and Anna Parnell, *The Tale of a Great Sham*, edited with an introduction by Dana Hearne (Dublin, 1986).

Context for Parnell's career can be found in D. A. Thornley, *Isaac Butt and Home Rule* (London, 1964), Conor Cruise O'Brien *Parnell and His Party, 1880–90* (2nd edn, Oxford 1964), Paul Bew, *Land and the National Question in Ireland, 1858–82* (Dublin, 1978), Samuel Clark, *Social Origins of the Irish Land War*

(Princeton, NJ, 1979), Alan O'Day, *The English Face of Irish Nationalism: Parnellite Involvement in British Politics, 1880–86* (Dublin, edns 1977–94), *Parnell and the First Home Rule Episode, 1884–87* (Dublin, 1986), and *Irish Home Rule, 1867–1921* (Manchester, 1998), Patrick Maume, *The Long Gestation: Irish Nationalist Life, 1891–1918* (Dublin, 1999), Alvin Jackson, *Home Rule: An Irish History, 1800–2000* (London, edns 2003–4) and *The Ulster Party: Irish Unionists in the House of Commons, 1884–1911* (Oxford, 1989), Patrick Buckland, *Irish Unionism: vol. 1: The Anglo-Irish and the New Ireland, 1885–1922* (Dublin, 1972) and *Irish Unionism: vol. 2: Ulster Unionism and the Origins of Northern Ireland, 1886–1922* (Dublin, 1973), James Loughlin, *Gladstone, Home Rule and the Ulster Question, 1882–93* (Dublin, 1986) and *The British Monarchy and Ireland: 1800 to the Present* (Cambridge, 2007), Ambrose Macaulay, *The Holy See, British Policy and the Plan of Campaign in Ireland, 1885–93* (Dublin, 2002), Owen McGee, *The IRB: The Irish Republican Brotherhood, from the Land League to Sinn Féin* (Dublin, 2005), Laurence Marley, *Michael Davitt: Freelance Radical and Frondeur* (Dublin, 2007), James H. Murphy, *Abject Loyalty: Nationalism and Monarchy in Ireland During the Reign of Queen Victoria* (Washington, DC and Cork, 2001) and *Ireland: A Social, Cultural and Literary history, 1791–1891* (Dublin, 2003), Thomas J. Morrissey, *William J. Walsh, Archbishop of Dublin, 1841–1921, No Uncertain Voice* (Dublin, 2000), F. S. L. Lyons, *John Dillon: A Biography* (London, 1968), Matthew J. Kelly, *The Fenian Ideal and Irish Nationalism, 1882–1916* (Woodbridge, 2006), Carla King, *Michael Davitt* (Dundalk, 1999), Marie-Louise Legg, *Newspapers and Nationalism: The Irish Provincial Press, 1850–1892* (Dublin, 1998), Emmet Larkin, *The Roman Catholic Church and the Emergence of the Modern Irish Political System, 1874–1878* (Dublin, 1996), *The Roman Catholic Church and the Creation of the Modern Irish State, 1878–86* (Dublin, 1976), *The Roman Catholic Church and the Plan of Campaign, 1886–88* (Cork, 1978), and *The Roman Catholic Church and the Fall of Parnell, 1888–91* (Liverpool, 1981), Joel A. Hollander, *Coloured Political Lithographs as Irish Propaganda: Warrior Artists and the Battle for Home Rule, 1879–1886* (Lewiston, NY, 2007), Philip J. Bull, *Land, Politics and Nationalism: A Study of the Irish Land Question* (Dublin, 1996), Malcolm Brown, *The Politics of Irish literature from Thomas Davis to W. B. Yeats* (London, edns 1972–3), T. N. Brown, *Irish-American Nationalism, 1870–1890* (Philadelphia, 1966), Frank Thompson, *The End of Liberal Ulster: Land Agitation and Land Reform, 1868–1886* (Belfast, 2001), L. P. Curtis, jr, *Coercion and Conciliation in Ireland, 1880–92: A Study in Conservative Unionism* (Princeton, NJ, 1963), Joseph V. O'Brien, *William O'Brien and the Course of Irish Politics, 1881–1918* (Berkeley, CA, 1976), Sally Warwick-Haller, *William O'Brien and the Irish Land War* (Dublin, 1990), Margaret O'Callaghan, *British High*

Politics and a Nationalist Ireland: Criminality, Land and the Law under Forster and Balfour (Cork, 1994), James J. O'Shea, *Priest, Politics and Society in Post-Famine Ireland: A Study of County Tipperary 1850–1891* (Dublin, 1983), Michael Winstanley, *Ireland and the Land Question 1800–1922* (London, 1984), Donald E. Jordan, jr, *Land and Popular Politics in Ireland: County Mayo From the Plantation to the Land War* (Cambridge, 1994), W. E. Vaughan, *Landlords and Tenants in Mid-Victorian Ireland* (Oxford, 1994), Brian M. Walker, *Ulster Politics: The Formative Years, 1868–1886* (Belfast, 1990), Senia Pašeta, *Before the Revolution: Nationalism, Social Change and Ireland's Catholic Elite, 1879–1922* (Cork, 1999), Eugene J. Doyle, *Justin McCarthy* (Dundalk, 1996), and T. W. Moody, *Davitt and Irish Revolution, 1846–82* (Oxford, 1982). K. Theodore Hoppen, *Elections, Politics, and Society in Ireland, 1832–1885* (Oxford, 1985), Tom Garvin, *The Evolution of Irish Nationalist Politics* (Dublin, edns 1981–2005), D. George Boyce (ed.), *The Revolution in Ireland, 1879–1923* (Dublin, 1988) and Eugenio F. Biagini, *British Democracy and Irish Nationalism 1876–1906* (Cambridge, 2007) contain much relevant material. A set of documents can be found in Noel Kissane, *Parnell: A Documentary History* (Dublin, 1991) and Michael De Nie (ed.), *Lives of Victorian Political Figures, Part II Vol. 2: Charles Stewart Parnell* (London, 2008). Katherine Wood O'Shea [Parnell], *Charles Stewart Parnell: His Love Story and Political Life* (London, edns 1914–2005; 2 vols) is indispensable.

Useful essays can be found in D. George Boyce and Alan O'Day (eds), *The Making of Modern Irish History: Revisionism and the Revisionist Controversy* (London, edns 1996–7); *Defenders of the Union: A Survey of British and Irish Unionisms since 1801* (London, 2001), *Ireland in Transition, 1867–1921* (London, 2004), *The Ulster Crisis, 1885–1921* (London and Basingstoke, 2005) and *Gladstone and Ireland: Politics, Religion and Nationality in the Victorian Age* (London and Basingstoke, 2010). Reprints of germane academic articles are in Alan O'Day (ed.), *Reactions to Irish Nationalism, 1865–1914* (London, 1987) and N. C. Fleming and Alan O'Day (eds), *Ireland and Anglo-Irish Relations: Critical Essays*, vols I and II (Aldershot, 2008).

Valuable general treatments of the period are Jeremy Smith, *Britain and Ireland: From Home Rule to Independence* (Harlow, 2000), Alvin Jackson, *Ireland 1798–1998: Politics and War* (Oxford, edns 1999–2003), D. George Boyce, *Ireland, 1828–1923* (Oxford, 1992), *Nineteenth-Century Ireland: The Search for Stability* (Dublin, edn 2005), and *Nationalism in Ireland* (4th edn, London, 2002), Alan J. Ward, *The Irish Constitutional Tradition: Responsible Government and Modern Ireland, 1782–1992* (Washington, DC and Blackrock, County Dublin, edns 1994–5), K. Theodore Hoppen, *Ireland since 1800* (London, 2nd edn, 1998–9), R. F. Foster, *Modern Ireland, 1600–1972* (London, edns 1989–2002), Paul Bew,

Ireland: The Politics of Enmity, 1789–2006 (Oxford, 2007). and Pauric Travers, *Settlements and Divisions: Ireland, 1870–1922* (Dublin, 1988). Chapters by R. V. Comerford in W. E. Vaughan (ed.), *A New History of Ireland*, VI: *Ireland under the Union, II: 1870–1921* (Oxford, 1996) provide a succinct overview of the period.

Index